MAKE THE WORLD YOUR RUNWAY

*Top Model Secrets for Everyday
Confidence and Success*

LIRIS CROSSE

Make the World Your Runway: Top Model Secrets for
Everyday Confidence and Success
Copyright © 2018 by Liris Crosse
Liris Crosse Publishing

www.lirisc.com

booklirisc@gmail.com

Editing and typesetting: Inksnatcher.com
Cover design: Camden Lane Creative Agency

Ordering Information: Quantity sales. Special discounts
are available on quantity purchases by corporations,
associations, and others. For details, contact the author at
the email address above.

Make the World Your Runway: Top Model Secrets for
Everyday Confidence and Success/Liris Crosse
ISBN-13: 978-0-9976997-2-2

This book is dedicated to my mother, Delois Crosse, for all the poise she exhibits and has given me throughout life. Also, I dedicate this to my father, Rev. St. George Crosse, who always boosted my self-esteem since I was a baby and told me I could achieve anything I put my mind to do.

ACKNOWLEDGMENTS

"Thank you" is one of the most beautiful gifts you can give with your words, and yes, I have a few I need to give out. This book has been a whirlwind of a journey I sometimes struggled to get done, but because of God, I crossed the finish line! Thank you, God, for focusing me, giving me the right words to write, and pushing me when I wanted to throw in the towel.

Thank you to my amazing parents, Rev. St. George and Delois Crosse, who are my biggest fans and who are the reason why I make the world my runway today. I love you and appreciate your support always. To my amazing big sister, Karin Haysbert. You have truly been my biggest help with this project, from coaching me on writing to helping me pull the resources together to make this great! I am thankful for your wisdom always.

To my best friend, Christy Baldwin, who, when I told her I was going to write a book, did what she always does and encouraged me. Thanks for always being in my corner, and thank you for your public relations work to make this project a success. To William Henry Rawls and Pervis Taylor, thank you for being two mighty men I can rely on and for being the peace amid my storms. Love you.

To my makeup artist, Christopher Michael, and my hairstylist, Yancey Edwards, thanks for beautifying me on the outside so my inner beauty could shine even more for this book cover and in my modeling career over the years. Thanks to my agency, Dorothy Combs Models, who help me make the world my runway with every booking by impacting the fashion world. Thanks to my book cover photographer, Ananta Cuffe (@thnwblk-) for bringing my vision to life. You survived a serious car accident, and I'm grateful to have you here to complete this and to call you my friend.

To my nieces, Olivia and Octavia Haysbert, and my nephew, Malcolm Bulls, I love you all so much, and because I know you are watching, you've helped me push to be a better role model. Also, to my closest cousin, Iris Crosse, thanks for always rooting me on.

To those in ministry who have prayed for me or spoken into my life, I just want to thank you for your wisdom and the encouragement to keep going: Markita D. Collins, Dr. A. R. Bernard, Prophet Herman Mitchell, Prophet Darnell Craig, Prophet Javon Maule, and Dr. Tamarrah Tarver. I so appreciate you.

Thanks to my Liris Loves who have followed and supported my career for years! Thanks to my new *Project Runway* fans who inspired me to pen this book! Welcome to my journey.

Liris Crosse

CONTENTS

FOREWORD

I love telling people that Liris Crosse and I met on a bus. We did. This was day one of *Project Runway*'s sixteenth season, and our bond immediately formed. We were sequestered on a custom *Project Runway* bus on a makeshift soundstage, along with fifteen other models and Heidi Klum. For the first time in the history of the show, I actually met the models before meeting the designers.

Season 16 was our seminal "models of all sizes" season. The season 16 designers, sequestered elsewhere, knew nothing about this. Our exit from the bus was to be the big reveal to them: sixteen gorgeous models ranging in size from 2 to 22. You may think that staging this reveal would be relatively simple, but few things on *Runway* are. In what order do we exit the bus? Who stands where? Who's next to whom? Where do Heidi and I stand so we don't block the models? Keep in mind that there are eighteen of us, which in a multiple camera shot constitutes a lot of people! Well, we rehearsed and rehearsed and rehearsed: exit the bus, walk to each of our designated spots, be presented to the designers, and return to the bus. We did this over and over until the director was satisfied he had a clean take. And I have to add that the lowest step exiting the bus was quite high, so there was a considerable stretch to the pavement. I was grateful I wasn't in stilettos like everyone else!

Given this protracted rehearsal, there was plenty of time on that first day for us all to get to know each other. Owing to happenstance, Liris was seated across the aisle from me. (I have to say that as gorgeous as she is on camera, she's breathtaking in person.) She reminded me that we had worked together before: she walked in the finale collection of season 14 winner, Ashley Tipton. We chatted and laughed and became a little too boisterous—the director had to tell us to be quiet! I knew from that moment that we would be great colleagues. I could also tell from her interaction with the fifteen other models that she would have an important leadership role among them. Indeed, she did.

To be perfectly candid, until season 16 I really didn't care who the models were or which ones were eliminated versus which ones remained. I barely interacted with them; they barely had a voice, and other than facial features and skin and hair color differences, they were practically interchangeable. Season 16 changed all of that. The models had voices and we heard them—during the consultations with designers, the fittings, the Model Mirror, and the presentation of the fashion designs to the judges. Liris and her peer models aren't mannequins; they're bodies and souls with fierce opinions and sets of strong beliefs, and they express those opinions and beliefs, with Liris being one of the more thoughtful and diplomatic among them.

Liris is a stalwart advocate for being who you are. In her words, *Own it!* This philosophy has multiple dimensions. Owning who you are means harnessing and maximizing the qualities and attributes you possess—physical presence, experience in the world, passions and influences, role models and mentors. I once heard another model ask Liris if there was anything in her life she would change. Without missing a beat, she responded, "No, nothing. Everything I've experienced, whether it's good or bad, celebratory or tragic, has made me who I am. Think about it: if we alter anything in our past, it changes who we are. That's not a positive thing to dwell on." How inspirational!

I've learned so much from Liris. Her positivity is contagious. It lifts the room. It makes you feel physically buoyant. During design consultations and fittings, her guidance to the designers had me spellbound. She'd tell them that designing for a woman with curves requires an amended conceptual process, that is, it's not about sizing up. Silhouette, proportion, and fit are the key factors for a successful look, the look being the combination of design + model. What's a design without a model, other than static clothes? And she tutored me on the term "plus size."

While waiting backstage before our first season 16 fashion show, Liris, Jazmine, and Monique were standing next to me. I said, "May I ask a favor of you? We must come up with an alternative to the term "plus size." It's pejorative. Let's spend this season finding a new term." Liris led. Gesturing to her fellow models, she said, "Actually, we like it. We believe it's the right term. If the world thinks it's pejorative, then we need to change the world." Her assertion rocked me from my foundation. And she converted me into a vocal advocate!

Make the World Your Runway is an advocacy too. It's an advocacy for *you*. Immerse yourself in the rallying spirit and extraordinary experience of Liris Crosse. You will learn how to own who you are and celebrate that ownership.

Own It and *Make It Work*!

Tim Gunn

Fashion consultant, television personality, fashion mentor on *Project Runway,* actor, voice actor, author

PREFACE

Wow! I finally did it. I wrote my first book! Birthing this book has been a labor of love, and I am so glad you have chosen to join me on this journey. My hope is that as you read its pages, my words will sink into your heart and help you to build your confidence to live the joyful life of success you desire.

The idea to write this book came to me after completing season 16 of *Project Runway*. It was such an exhilarating time for me because the fans are simply tremendous. As I engaged with the show's fanbase on social media, so many shared about how my confidence shined through every time I hit the runway or spoke in the model mirror segments. I would get comments like "If only I could bottle up your confidence" or "I wish I had your self-esteem." It got me thinking of how much we affect others just by being who we are and by how we show up in the world daily.

I have always thought of the world as a canvas that we paint with the beautiful colors of who we are. I believe that is why we are all unique: unique in race, size, gender, background, and experience. What's so magical is that it's those differences that make us so beautiful. I thought of how I approach the runway and how I approach life, which have so many parallels. As I reflected on my life, I thought I'd share with you:

— how walking in your purpose and your passion gives birth to confidence

— that preparation will separate you from average and put you on a higher playing field of success

— the power of first impressions and how to make sure that your presentation internally and externally put you in the best position to prosper

— how to dress for success

— the importance of keeping your energy pure so that your presence is positive and attractive wherever you go

— that no matter how many times you feel like giving up, how to persist until you succeed and build your self-belief

— that recognizing and standing in your power is a key to success

— how to receive support when you need it and give it to others through partnerships

No one makes it to the top alone.

This long, beautiful career and even more amazing life has taught me so many lessons.

Those experiences became me, the me you saw blessed with such confidence on *Project Runway* and the hundreds and thousands of other photo shoots, television shows, and movie appearance over the years.

I wrote this book, bottled it up, so everyone could share a piece of my confidence canvas! Confidence is at the heart of most successes in life. So many wonderful, triumphant things will never happen in life if you lack confidence. I want to help you to get it. You deserve to live in confidence!

I have always wanted the best for others. I'm that friend who looks at people and gives them a makeover in my head for their physical and emotional selves, so I pray this book adds to the amazing person who you already are. May it give you the boost or fine-tuning of the brilliance already inside that just needed a friendly nudge to come out.

Your life makeover begins today. You deserve to live your best life so you can make the world your runway too! The world needs what only you can give. Turn the page to begin the journey in 5, 4, 3, 2, 1...

Love,

Liris C

"The runway symbolizes something in society that's very intimidating to women."
– Tyra Banks

"The most alluring thing a woman can have is confidence."
– Beyoncé Knowles

"Success is only meaningful and enjoyable if it feels like your own."
– Michelle Obama

INTRODUCTION

Confidence. Even the word is full of power and vitality. It's a word that makes you sit up straighter and walk with your head lifted higher. On the runway, confidence is key! All eyes are on you, and it's your moment to shine to bring forth a specific result. On the runway of life, eyes are on you too. There are people who are looking to you for that very special thing that only you can bring forth. To do that with a sense of joy, you must have confidence.

So, let's define it.

Confidence is belief in oneself. It is defined as belief in one's powers. Confidence is belief in your abilities. When you are confident, you trust yourself. You believe in your own worth, value, and reliability. Confidence is a feeling of certainty that arises from an appreciation of yourself. If there is anyone whom we must have confidence in, it's ourselves! It's nice for others to believe in us, but we must believe in ourselves even more.

What I have learned is that confidence is crucial in living the full, rich lives that we are destined to live. Life is supposed to be fun. It's supposed to bring us great growth and joy in the process.

Success Is Yours!

Success is yours. You were born to be a success, but what does that mean? Success can be defined as the accomplishment of your goals. For some, it is the attainment of wealth, power, position, popularity, or fame. Do you know what success means to you? If you don't, you can spend your lifetime chasing after someone else's definition of success. When we're not clear about what we want from life, we end up living someone else's idea of how our lives should be.

I believe success is when we live the lives that we were sent here to live. Know this. You are an infinite, divine being, and nothing is impossible for you. You are more than enough to fulfill your purpose and to live a successful life of joy, peace, and blessings. Success is making the world your runway. The world is your stage. Success is allowing yourself to fully be who you are. It's putting your gifts and graces on display on the runway of life so that all the world can benefit from the blessing called *you*. With that said, the foundation of our confidence and success must be rooted in our purpose. Let's talk about it!

"Nothing is more beautiful than a confident woman who doesn't pretend to be something she's not."
– Unknown

"You know you are on the road to success if you would do your job and not be paid for it."
– Oprah Winfrey

"Modeling chose me, I didn't choose modeling."
– Tyra Banks

— 1 —

LIVE IN YOUR PURPOSE

HOW DOES WALKING IN YOUR PURPOSE give birth to confidence and success? It's by walking it out.

WALK IT OUT

I have always wanted to be a model. From the time I was very young, I remember being interested in fashion and hair and design. I would pose in front of mirrors and prance around the house in dresses and my mom's heels. In fact, my first shoot was actually performed by my sister, Karin, and my older cousin Brian.

It was a hot, summer day. I guess they were bored
and decided to have a little fun by using me as a baby
Barbie doll. (Hint: I'd love to have a "Liris Barbie doll!")
They put makeup on me, adorned me in an iris blue
cotton dress with a big, flowing skirt. Then my sister
placed a portable fan on the floor and tilted it upward to
make the skirt poof up like Marilyn Monroe's iconic
white-dress, flying-skirt scene from 1954. She still
laughs to this day about how, at two or three years old, I
pouted my ruby red lips, raising my arms in the air
posing for the camera. I still have those pictures.

Your Purpose Is IN You

How is it that even as a toddler I knew what I loved to
do? Even more, I already knew *what* to do. It's because
your purpose is in you. I just did what came naturally to
me. There is a supreme confidence that comes when you
know you are doing what you are and being who you are.
Like Tyra Banks said, "Modeling chose me, I didn't
choose modeling." I didn't consciously reason it out. It
was what came to me as a child with ease. I came here, to
Earth, with it in me already. It knew it in my bones.
Because of that, I could go through the many trials and
difficulties, and trust that things would get better, turn
around, and eventually work out. Nothing that we are
called to do will come without difficulties. It's a part of
the human existence, but when you know you are
operating according to a calling that is higher and

greater than this human experience, it strengthens you to move forward. It emboldens you to step up and show out.

"There's no greater gift than to honor your life's calling. It's why you were born and how you become most truly alive."
– Oprah Winfrey

GLANCE AT THE GLIMPSES

How do you find your purpose? Look at the glimpses of your calling. Sometimes, we can stifle a child's purpose because we are not seeing them in the full scope of who they are. We might say, "Why does she talk so much? Why is she always playing in my makeup? Why is she always messing with my hair stuff? Why is it that every time I go into his room, he is dribbling a basketball in my house, making all that noise, or he's sleeping with that basketball? Every time I take him to church, that boy always ends up playing on the microphone! Why is she always taking things apart and trying to put things together? She's always breaking up my things," and on and on. Maybe that's the next engineer, singer, hairstylist, makeup artist, dancer, basketball player, preacher, or teacher! The list doesn't stop! But how many dreams have died because someone unknowingly crushed a child's creative genius?

Many times, our purpose is shown in glimpses in our childhood. Our calling calls us, but we are sometimes seen as being bad or disruptive, when we could be just trying to figure out our own brilliance. It has been said that "every child is born a genius," and then well-meaning adults, culture, society, and others talk us out of our own purpose and calling. Not you! Don't stand for this another day!

What are you called to do and to be? What do you really enjoy doing? Who are you? What is your divine purpose? If you feel unsure, it's okay. Everyone doesn't know as clearly as I did, but I promise you that there have been glimpses of it that God has been showing you. Here's where you have to do a little investigative work on yourself so you can begin to make the world your runway.

Runway Action Plan—Ask Yourself

Get to a quiet place alone. Grab a journal and something to write with. Ask yourself these questions, and write the answers in your journal. Continue to add to it as you go through this book. Write any ideas or thoughts that surface for you along the way.

As a child, what things did you love to do?

— What things came naturally for you?

— What did you see yourself doing when you grew up?

— What did people say you were really good at?

— What were the things you were scolded for?

— What were the compliments teachers gave you?

— What do your friends tell you that you're so great at?

— What do people thank you for helping them with?

— What do you feel most at home doing?

— What do you like to do that you would do for free?

STAND IN YOUR GENIUS

You must be willing to STAND in your genius just like I stand in mine when I pose at the end of the runway. Embrace your gifting. You must be and do what your heart calls for. That gives you the confidence that will lead to success when you act on it. You must take action. Here's something I always share about standing in your genius with the participants in my Life of a Working Model Boot Camp. To learn more about it, go to www.loawmbc.com.

> My dad never wanted me to say woulda, coulda, shoulda, so even though our family is known for having doctors and lawyers, he gave me the chance to pursue my dreams of modeling. Sometimes parents try to box their children in because of their limited scope of what they have achieved, not realizing that you should allow your children to try many things to find their purpose. When people operate in their purpose,

it allows them to live their best life, even when it's a struggle. Stop forcing kids to do what you want them to do instead of what they were born to do. Stop limiting them because of your own fears.

— Liris

Think about this statement. This doesn't just apply to how family may have limited you, but also, how have you limited yourself? Have you allowed others' beliefs of what they want for you to stop you from fulfilling what you feel is your God-given purpose, hopes, and dreams? Have you used that as an excuse not to stretch yourself, not to dream bigger?

What's Your Vision?

"The only thing worse than being blind is having sight but no vision."
– Helen Keller

"If you don't have a vision for the future, then your future is threatened to be a repeat of the past."
– A. R. Bernard

Do you have a vision for your life? If you don't, your life might be on repeat. As Helen Keller said, you can have natural sight, but if you do not have a vision for your life, it's much worse than being physically blind. I love her story. She did not let her physical disabilities of being deaf and blind disable her life. She went within herself and found her talents and gifts and used them. No excuses.

What's your vision? How do you see your life unfolding? I had a vision. I could see where I was going. Vision is sensing with the eyes and seeing beyond your eyes. True vision is an element of great FAITH. It is looking past the current circumstances and seeing what really exists beyond the illusion of today's "failures." Vision creates power in your life because it allows you to see the unseen. It helps you create in the now what exists in the future.

There were many times in my life when I had to draw from the reservoir of confidence that only vision could supply. As a little girl, I would daydream about traveling around the world and seeing beautiful places. My mother always said that I needed to marry a rich man because I had expensive tastes. I guess I thought that way because, as a child, I believed my father was rich. I felt like I should have the best. I created a place in my mind for having the best. I still do.

Vision Pulls You through the Hard Times

Although I felt like a shining princess as a little girl, it wasn't always true in my reality as I stepped into my career years later. I vividly remember the years of hard work and extreme struggle. Somewhere I believed that it had to be hard. I picked up the "starving artist" mentality and had to "rob Peter to pay Paul." I have lived in places that my family never knew about and would have never allowed me to stay in, but I was determined to make it on my own. I remember sleeping on bags of clothes because I didn't have a bed. I can recall times when I lived in a basement apartment that had rats—not mice, rats. I lived below the poverty line for several years. Yes, I've been on the mountaintop, but I have spent a fair share of time below the valley's floor. So, if things have ever been really hard for you, know that I've been there too.

I have felt like quitting countless times. Maybe you have felt like this. *Why does it have to be so hard to do the things that I love? Why is it so challenging to do what I know I'm made for? Why does it seem like the world is against me?* I have struggled with those feelings too. What has helped to pull me through the inevitable slumps is vision. I had a vision. Until I saw on the outside the vision that had been burned in my heart on the inside, I made a commitment to keep going.

"There is one rule, though: once you discover your truth, you have to go all in. Fully.
Every single chip."
– Kamal Ravikant

"Commitment unlocks the doors of imagination, allows vision, and gives us the 'right stuff'

to turn our dreams into reality."
— James Womack

YOU MUST COMMIT

When you make commitments, especially those you make to yourself, it can bring confidence to you almost instantly. It allows you to trust and believe in yourself. Make commitments and keep them. No excuses! Be a person who keeps your word with yourself over and over again. When you can rely on yourself, it builds self-confidence more than anything else. Additionally, you have to go all in with the vision for your life. Your vision will give you the motivation to keep moving. It's the visualization of your big "why"—the motive or the reason for why you don't give up. We will talk more about that later in chapter 5, "Fueling Your Passion and Persistence."

Your vision will help you move beyond your comfort zone. Sometimes we get it mixed up. We think that the comfort zone is comfortable. No, it is just familiar. Don't allow other people's comfort zones to become yours. Refuse to let their fears keep you from walking in the confidence and success you were created for. To make the world your runway, you must understand that living your dreams will require you to do things that are out of the norm, unfamiliar, and downright scary sometimes. That's okay! I did not come out of the womb knowing how to build a successful career in the modeling and entertainment industry, but because I had a vision for where I was going and refused to give up, the "how to do it" showed up step by step. Trust that your Creator is always trying to lead you in the path of fulfilling your purpose with the greatest joy.

USE YOUR IMAGINATION TO CREATE SUCCESS

"If you can dream it, you can do it."
– Walt Disney

"Your imagination is everything. It is the preview of life's coming attractions."
– Albert Einstein

To give life to the vision within you, you must use your imagination. Your imagination is EVERYTHING! Your life may not yet look like how you desire it to be right now, but you can change it with the power of your own imagination. Long before I walked the runways, worked with the world's top designers, graced any magazine covers, or modeled in worldwide company campaigns, I saw it in my own imagination. I visualized myself walking the runways. I heard the cheers of the audience. I envisioned myself being interviewed and hosting large events. I saw myself in exotic locations working for impressive clients and doing shoots with the world's top photographers. I watched myself on the billboards and on TV shows and in movies on the screens in my mind first. I was previewing what was coming to me.

You are no different from me. You can do the same. Honestly, you must do the same to walk in confidence and success. Your imagination is a foretaste of your future. As Einstein so eloquently said, "[Imagination] is the preview of your life's coming attractions." Have you ever watched a movie trailer and gotten so excited about it that you couldn't wait to see it? That's what happened to me when I saw the previews of *Black Panther*. I was so excited to see these African superheroes. Superheroes who looked like me gracing the silver screen in a major motion picture, receiving such major press, thrilled me. It had been a long time since I'd been this enthusiastic about a film. I got my tickets well in advance and planned a whole weekend around the premiere. It turned out to be even greater than what I had expected.

How much more must we do the same for our own lives? When was the last time you were so engrossed in the vision for your own life that it caused you to make plans to receive the success you were envisioning? It prompted you to take action. It propelled you into your dreams.

"Shoot for the moon. Even if you miss, you'll land among stars!"
– Les Brown

11

GIVE YOURSELF SPACE TO DREAM BIG!

Giving yourself space to dream stretches you. Be a BIG dreamer. Les Brown famously said, "Shoot for the moon. Even if you miss, you'll land among stars!" In other words, dream big. Even if you fall short, you're still way more ahead than if you had played it safe. And why do we play it safe? Often, it's because we have been hurt and disappointed in the past, things didn't work out like we imagined, or we didn't get the support from others we thought we would—and we're tired. Trust me, I've been there.

Can I encourage you? Today is a new day. Even if it didn't work in the past, try again. Big dreams take faith and determination to manifest. If it didn't, everyone would be living large. There is a Bible passage that says, "Many are called but few are chosen," which means that although we are called and have the capability to succeed, few choose to do what it takes to have it. Also, we often underestimate our abilities and what is even possible for us. With all of my own visions and imaginations, I still leave room for God to give me dreams even bigger and better than I could imagine.

Sometimes we are afraid to dream big. We get scared because we don't see the way to making the dream happen. That is not our part. We must simply open ourselves up to dream as big as we can and then allow things to fall into place in the best possible way for us.

We must learn to trust, to listen to the whispers, and follow them. Besides, what do you have to lose? If you don't push yourself, you won't grow. You'll lessen your impact. You'll decrease your own joy and fulfillment. Life is about growth and expansion. Dream BIG!

> *"Create the highest, grandest vision possible for your life, because you become what you believe."*
> *– Oprah Winfrey*

WRITE THE VISION

Write those dreams down. I remember that as a child I would dream about days when I would fly to Paris for lunch and a fashion show. I would write these dreams in my journal. Do you journal? It's a great way to help get the dreams inside of you out. Write them down. Writing those dreams down gives them life. It also makes them more concrete. It actually lets the world know that you are serious about them. Maybe you've heard the words, "Write the vision. Make it plain." Write your dreams. Write your visions. Make them plain to *you* so you can open yourself up to hear what your next steps are to successfully fulfill them. Make it plain to *others* so they can identify how to help you to achieve them.

STOP LIMITING YOURSELF BECAUSE OF FEAR

Let's talk a little more about fear. How does pushing past your perceived limitations overcome fear? Know this: to build runway confidence, you must push past your fears. Literally every time I'm about to walk the runway, my heart starts to jump out of my chest! It did it every time on *Project Runway* too! You will often have an opportunity to feel fear, but you don't have to let it stop you. Turn that fear into excitement. That's exactly what I do, with that ball of nerves, right before I step out on the stage. Pause. Take some deep breaths. Center yourself. Let the fear fuel you to courageously step out in faith. Stop limiting yourself because of your own fear, and refuse to limit yourself because of the fears of others. Be like me, and step out there anyway!

Fear is a normal response to a perceived threat. It will rise up in an attempt to try to keep you safe. It is also why other people will sometimes tell you that you need to play it safe. They will tell you that you need to get a good, safe job, a good government job, or one where you have many guarantees. While there is nothing wrong with having a career that includes a job, there is something wrong with it if you know deep within you, you are supposed to be doing something else.

Maybe you were born to write songs that inspire people to love one another. Perhaps you were created to paint murals that inspire imagination. You could be here to be a sculptor who creates works of art that celebrate the wonder of the human body. Maybe you were born to have a public relations agency that would help businesses that have gone through an image nightmare to regain integrity and trust with their clients. There are so many ways we limit ourselves because of what our parents want or what society has deemed as what we should do.

Runway Action Plan—Commit

I need to pause here. Before we go any further. I must ask you something. This is your life. Every decision that you make or fail to make is creating your existence. Will you make a full-out commitment to go all in to yourself and to all the people whose lives are primed to be blessed by your gifts? I know that you can, but will you? If so, please fill this in below now:

I, _____, make a commitment to use my gifts of

_____
_____ to make the world a better place and to live a joyful, fulfilled life. I promise to dream big. I promise to keep going no matter what. I commit to learning what I came here to learn. I decide to love and be loved. I'll make adjustments when I need to, but I'll never give up. This is my commitment, and I'm staying the course.

In Truth,

_____

Your Name & Date

What Is Your Heart and Soul Burning to Do?

Let's keep going. My heart and my soul burned to model. When I was in school, my parents really didn't allow me to do that much with modeling. Education is very important to my family. My dad is West Indian. His family immigrated to America so the children could receive an excellent university education. Needless to say, most of my aunts and uncles have multiple advanced degrees and have successful professional careers.

My mom, who is from the South, was one of the first people in her family to attend and graduate from college. This is what she knew as the path to success. Mom was very afraid of my going into modeling. She worried about how I would be able to live and take care of myself. She had been told all her life that the path to success and security was in getting a college education and a good, safe job with benefits. That was not modeling at all.

When I graduated from high school, my mom wanted me to go to college so that I could have a backup plan. I totally understand why she felt that way. But after going to conventions with Model Search America and seeing the callbacks that I received from various agencies that were interested in me, she lightened up, released some of her fears, and along with my father, gave her blessing for me to move to New York and pursue my modeling dreams. I never looked back!

Go for It!

Are you letting the fears of others stop you? If you are, you are telling the universe you're not ready for your dreams. No limits! Forge ahead anyway. When you accept that fear is a necessary part of the process, you can show you are ready to move forward despite it and you won't allow fear to stop you. You might see—no, you *will* see—that most of your fears are unfounded. What's the worst that can happen? You'd die? You won't get out of life alive anyway, so you might as well live your life and go for your dreams now.

Somebody Is Waiting for You to Obey Your Calling

Let's close this chapter with this. Somebody is waiting for you to obey your calling. As we have discussed before, God speaks to us often in whispers, through the glimpses, and with different signs. However, it's up to us to obey what it is He is telling us to do. You just don't know who is watching you. Who is waiting to see you walk in your purpose so it can help them to build the belief to catapult themselves into theirs? Who may be affected by your obeying the call on your life?

17

Runway Story Time—I'm Scared, but I'll Do It

I love to play the game Words with Friends. I don't usually have a lot of conversation on it, but one day, I was playing the game with a gentleman who simply asked me how I was doing. I was having a really bad day, and I just said that I was doing alright. When I asked him how he was doing, he said, "I'm doing alright in spite of." Then he went on to tell me he had been battling pancreatic cancer.

Not too long ago, I lost a beloved uncle who battled cancer too. I am intimately acquainted with how difficult that can be, as I saw him fighting and clinging on to life before he transitioned. So here was this gentleman fighting cancer who was really concerned with how I was doing, and saw the silver lining in his own day.

Soon after, I was at my parents' house doing some cleaning, going through books. A book fell open to a section on natural cures for pancreatic cancer. My mind went immediately to this gentleman. I know that I heard God tell me to send him that information. "What?" I thought. "We don't really know each other. Will he think I'm strange?" I took pictures of it with my phone and sent it to him through Facebook anyway.

Time had passed, and about a month later I was on Words with Friends again and saw him. I asked him how he was doing. He told me he was doing much better, and he thanked me for sending him those pages. He had shown them to his doctors, they implemented what was on those pages, and he had gone from stage 4 pancreatic cancer to stage 2.

This makes me want to weep. Can I tell you that I was afraid? I didn't want to appear weird to him, but I just obeyed. Who knows, perhaps my obedience in sharing that information helped to extend his life so he could have more time to spend with his beautiful daughter. Be obedient to your calling, not just in what you see as your purpose but in your everyday life. That is purpose too. I often think that our purpose for even connecting online could have been just for that reason.

There was another young woman that I knew only vaguely through Facebook; we are Facebook friends. I did know from seeing her posts she had recently given birth to twins. One night, I was scrolling through Facebook, and I heard to send her a message. But it was two thirty in the morning! Now I really felt uncomfortable. It was early, and we're not close friends. But I did what I felt nudged to do, and I sent her a word of encouragement. I let her know that she was more than enough for all that she was going through. She messaged me right back and told me she was up walking through the house crying, and she so needed that encouragement. She had not told anyone what she was going through. She thanked me for my obedience.

I didn't know what she was experiencing. She could have been in the throes of total exhaustion or postpartum depression. I just know what I heard, and although I was afraid to seem "churchy" to this almost stranger, I simply obeyed.

Here is my challenge for you. Stand in your purpose. Confidently move in your calling. You were made for this. You don't know who is attached to your greatness and your obedience to it. This is why you must operate on your highest level. This is why you have to move when you are directed to move, to stand up and share your brilliance with the world, and to be all that you were created to be.

Listen to the whispers. Stop second-guessing the voice of the Spirit in you. You have no idea whose life, whose livelihood, whose purpose, or whose freedom is attached to you. I was afraid. You may be too, but use that fear to push yourself forward. Whatever it is that God has called you to do, do it. You have no idea whose lives will be enriched because you stepped out on faith and started your design line or opened your child-care business or pursued your law degree. You don't know whose child will experience healing because you pushed past the fear of going to med school, became a doctor, and now use your healing hands to transform their lives.

Look around you. Your life and purpose have been attached to others too. Aren't you thankful they weren't too afraid to stand in their purpose and inspire you in yours? Return the favor, and be a blessing to the world. Your blessings are on the other side of your obedience.

Runway Action Plan—Create Your Vision Board

Probably many of you have already heard of and created vision boards. I believe it is a wonderful practice to help you to actually get a vision for your success. This is even a fun activity to do with your family or friends.

Whether you make it on poster board or in a lovely binder, get a variety of magazines, look for pictures, words, or phrases that make you dream bigger. Cut them out. Arrange them beautifully. Put your vision board in a place where you can see it daily. Look at your vision board, and then close your eyes and see yourself in the vision.

How would it feel to have what you see? Who is with you? What things are you saying? See yourself in the vision in full color. Use your imagination to get the full effect, to fully emotionally experience it. These are the things that create new tracks in your mind and help you to bring it to pass in your life.

I have done many vision boards over the years. Many of my biggest breakthroughs, greatest career connections, most glorious experiences, were first on my vision board. Set aside some time to make yours within the next few days. Write down the date when you will have it completed here: _____.

"The separation is in the preparation."
– Russell Wilson

"One important key to success is self-confidence.
An important key to self-confidence is
preparation."
– Arthur Ashe

"I feel that luck is preparation meeting
opportunity."
– Oprah

— 2 —

PREPARE FOR SUCCESS

PREPARATION IS TRULY A CONFIDENCE
BOOSTER, and it sets you up for success. It is the
process of putting things into proper order or condition.
It separates you from average and puts you on a higher
playing field. Preparation is getting ready for
something or someone. Just the act of preparing
yourself mentally, emotionally, and physically causes
your confidence to rise. It makes you feel like your
vision, your dreams, are about to happen.

We have all seen how a bird builds a nest. It starts by
gathering twigs, grass, leaves, mud, and even stones.

Many nests are made of any materials that the bird can find. The bird is building the nest in anticipation of something happening. They know they are about to lay an egg, and they need a safe place for the eggs and the baby birds to develop. What's coming your way? Raise your level of expectation! Sometimes, you too will have to use whatever is available to you until you can do better. That's fine. Start where you are, but prepare. Start building.

Preparation tells you and all the world that you are expecting things to happen. This helps to build a level of excitement and confidence in you. When I step out on the runway, trust me, I have prepared myself for that moment. As you step out onto the runway of life, if you want to experience the success that you desire, you will have to prepare too.

"If you fail to plan, you are planning to fail!"
– Benjamin Franklin

"A clear vision, backed by definite plans,
gives you a tremendous feeling of confidence
and personal power."
– Brian Tracy

"Proper planning and preparation
prevent poor performance."
– Old British Military Adage

PLAN YOUR RUNWAY LIFE

Planning is an easy way to build confidence that prepares you for success. It's simple. When you have a plan, you feel ready for whatever may happen. One of the things I do before I walk on the runway is plan how I'm going to sell the outfit with my strut and turns. That way, I can walk confidently and not look clueless. Of course, we know that almost anything can happen, but planning helps to take some of the stress out of situations, even if the unexpected occurs. Your mind is programmed to dislike the unknown. That's why fear holds so many of us back from fully living our lives. Planning is a simple confidence hack. It allows you to take fear out of the equation because it answers the "how" question. It makes some unknown things feel known. When you're able to see at least the next step toward where you're going, you feel less fearful and more confident.

As a working model, there are so many little things that I plan for that help to alleviate anxiety for me. It could be as simple as my planning in preparation for a shoot. I will usually get my eyebrows waxed beforehand so that I don't have to concern myself with a makeup artist whom I have never worked with messing up my brows. Think about it—no one wants that anxiety! What little things could you plan for in your daily life that will alleviate the unnecessary uneasiness you feel day to day?

Set Meaningful Goals

You may have heard it said that a dream without goals is merely a wish. A large part of your planning and preparation process is to set goals that move you toward the success you dream about. The only way to do that is to start with your big why. Author Simon Sinek says in his famous TED Talk, "Start with Why," and in his book entitled the same, "People do not buy what you do; they buy why you do it" (Portfolio/Penguin, 2009, 41). You cannot convey why you do it if you don't have a strong why behind what you do. This is how you set meaningful goals.

Sinek contends that emotions trump reason every time. Your goals must have strong, compelling, emotional reasons behind them, or they will have no substance. Truth be told, those types of goals don't usually involve money or possessions. They're often related to relationships and loved ones. For example, you might have the goal of losing twenty-five pounds. Why? Because you want to release some of the pressure on your joints. Why? Because it will allow you to lead a more active lifestyle. Why? Because you will have the energy to do the things you want to do. Why? Because you want to be able to enjoy spending your life and doing things that are fun with your grandchildren. Why? Because you had a great relationship with your grandparents and know how important they were in making you the person that you are today. That's your meaningful, big why. Family is a core value for you. Family relationships are extremely important to you. And being available to cultivate them is your why.

Runway Action Plan—Ask Yourself...

My vision boards are a visual representation of my end goals, but I also have various written goals in different areas of my life to lead me toward my end goals. Remember to search your heart to get your why, and let's explore the goals that support them. If you do not have goals for your life, you are probably living at the mercy of someone else who does. Yogi Berra once said, "If you don't know where you're going, you'll end up someplace else." How true.

Here are some things to consider so that you can plan and set meaningful goals for your life. Get your journal. Write the first things that come up for you. You can always add to them. In fact, I encourage you to.

— What are your spiritual goals? How do you want to grow spiritually? Why is that important to you?

— What are your emotional goals? What feelings do you want to have more of? More love? More joy? More peace? Why?

— What areas do you want to mature in? To be more forgiving? More steadfast? Keep your word with yourself and others more? Why?

— What are your intellectual goals? What things would you like to learn in this season of your life? Go back to school? Earn a degree? Complete a certification? Read more? Why?

— What are your physical goals? In what ways would you like to improve your health and fitness? More energy? Better rest and sleep? Improved eating habits? Why?

— What experiences would you like to have? Would you like to travel to each of the continents of the world? Would you like to swim with dolphins? Would you like to climb a mountain or backpack across a country? Would you like to learn a foreign language? To ski, to play golf, or to paint portraits? Think about what experiences would enrich your life and why.

— How would you like your relationships to be? Your love life? Your relationships with your extended family? Your friendships? Your co-workers or business associates? Why?

— What career goals do you have? Where would you like to see your career progressing toward in the next year? The next three years? What promotions do you desire? What increased income or salary would you like to receive? Business income? Business expansion? Why?

— What things would you like to do to contribute to your community? How would you like to leave your mark in the Earth? What do you want your legacy to be? Why?

I love this activity. Keep answering the questions, and keep asking yourself *why*. One thing I have always said is that in my lean years as well as my lavish years I have always made sure to have a life full of experiences. I have lived a rewarding, beautiful life. I'm so thankful to have met interesting people and to have traveled the world for work and for play, enjoying myself in the process.

PLEASE NOTE. *Your goals should never just be about money or career. You are a multifaceted person, and your life deserves goals that represent each area. Focus on your reasons why.*

Your Personal New Year

When should you plan these goals? New Year's? Right now? It's up to you. I plan my goals around my birthday. I call it my Personal New Year. My birthday is in

October, so by New Year's Day it is usually a check-in time for me to see where I am after a couple of months of resetting my goals. The choice is yours, but be like Nike and "Just Do It."

Runway Action Plan—Let's Check In

Did you take some quiet time alone to contemplate each of the above questions in the previous "Runway Action Plan" section? If you didn't, please stop and do it now. Write down the first things that come to mind. Don't linger over each one for more than two to three minutes. Actually time it. If you do linger too long, your fear mind might kick in and talk you out of it. The first answer is usually the most honest. Go through it completely, answer all the questions, and start to compose a plan.

With each area, what is one thing that you can do right now to move yourself toward those end goals?

Pick two or three things to focus on for the next 90 days and start moving. It doesn't have to be perfect. JUST MOVE!

"When you plan for success,
you usually have success."
– Liris

Be Prepared for Your Moment (and the Other Stuff That Happens)

There are times in life when you do have to prepare contingency plans as you confidently fulfill the steps to your dreams. This is not the same as a plan B that you run to at the slightest sign of difficulty. News flash! It's not going to work all the time. Accept that reality, and prepare for how you will mentally and emotionally forge forward through it, and make provisions for anything you can do to overcome any potential obstacles. This is simply being ready for situations that may occur within the process of life.

As a runway model, I'm always prepared for things that may happen on a shoot or in a runway show. I pack my model bag to ensure I am covered to the best of my ability. Recently I had an incident at a fashion show that illustrated this point.

"You can't just get ready.
You must stay ready."
– Liris

Runway Story Time

Most times when you are at a runway show, the client will have shoes they would like for you to wear with their garments. I don't always trust that their shoes will fit me correctly or will be comfortable throughout the entire day. Because of that, I always bring two of my own pairs of shoes with me for my runway shows. I was in Barcelona, Spain, for my client, Maggie Sottero, and so thankful to be the first black plus model to walk in Barcelona Bridal Week. For this particular show, I brought my favorite runway shoes with me. They are comfortable. They are lived in. They are simply the best. Recently, the strap had broken off the top one of them, and I fixed it prior to the show.

As I was out on the runway, I do my extra little turn, and the whole front strap across the toes of the shoe broke off. My foot actually hit the floor. Yikes! Thankfully, my dress was so long that it covered the whole ordeal, and no one was the wiser. I turned again, without changing my facial expression, and walked back down the runway on my tippy toes on one foot so that no one could see what was going on under the exquisite gown I was wearing.

Because I was prepared backstage, I was able to change into my second backup pair of runway shoes. Here's the kicker. No one else in the show was my size, and they didn't have shoes to fit me. I learned this lesson early on having to walk in shows with shoes that were one or more sizes too small. Imagine if I didn't have those shoes with me and would not have been able to finish the show.

Anything can happen. You must be prepared. The president of Maggie Sottero was sitting right there, on the front row, at the end of the runway. He didn't even realize that my whole shoe had broken off my foot. Never let them see you sweat. When I casually mentioned to him what happened and that it was all good because I had another pair of shoes, his reply was "Oh wow! That's great!" Others appreciate when you are prepared. Remember that.

In making the world your runway, you must be prepared because you never know who's watching you. You have no idea what opportunities are on the verge of appearing in your life. It has been said that success is where preparation and opportunity meet. What you don't want to happen is for opportunity to show up and find you not prepared for it. Be ready for your moment, and anything else that could happen, to the best of your ability at all times.

"The wise ask questions."
– Liris

"I'm determined, and I'm passionate and driven about whatever I commit myself to do. If I don't know something, I'm going to ask, and I've got no problems in asking questions. I never have. People ask me, 'Are you nervous when you go on the runway? You don't look it.' 'Yes, I am.'"
– Naomi Campbell

ASK QUESTIONS

There is one last thing I'd like to bring out here about your preparation for success. In order to plan and properly prepare for the special moments in life, you must ask questions. The wise ask questions. Sometimes we assume that we know exactly what is needed in a situation. Unfortunately, most assume incorrectly. Why not clear that up and just ask questions?

Everyone wants to win. Everyone wants to succeed. We have to get out of the mold of thinking that asking questions suggests you are "less than" because you don't know something. Sometimes that creeps in during childhood, especially in school. *Don't you dare raise your hand because those other kids will think you're stupid. You can't let anyone know you don't understand.* Why are you in school anyway? Obviously to learn. In school and in life, the wisest person asks questions, and lots of them.

When I prepare for a shoot, I will ask, "What is the hair look for this job?" My agent will send me reference photos from the client. Then, I will prepare my hair that way, whether it means getting a weave or wig that will ready me for the job. I always go to a job with short manicured nails in nude or pink. I try to do as much as I can in advance to make the post-production job as easy as possible for my client. I don't have to do that, but it sets me apart by going the extra mile. When you do, people want to work with you again and again.

"There is little traffic on the extra mile."
– Liris

Always give your best in all that you do. Go above and beyond. I give every client my very best. I treat the $1,500-a-day client just like the $15,000-a-day client with regard to my preparation. This gives me a competitive edge. More importantly, it gives me a sense of peace and confidence. It can do that for you too.

Runway Action Plan—Ask Yourself...

This is a mini pit stop. Really think about this.

— Do you make it easy for others to work with you, to live with you, or to be with you because you ask questions that allow you to show your best in every situation?

— Are you assuming things or expecting others to read your mind and then running into complications because of it?

— Stop wondering what your job, your supervisor, your spouse, or your friend wants, and simply ask. You have a right to ask and to understand. Give yourself and others this truth, and live in this truth.

PLAN TO BE ON TIME!!!

Are You Ready for Success?

Are you ready for all the great things you have been preparing for? How would we know? Do you have the posture of someone who's ready for business? If we watched your life, would it indicate that you are positioned for your success? One area that tells a lot about a person is their *punctuality*. Punctuality shows that you are ready for life's opportunities.

It has been said the majority of success is in simply showing up. In addition, I contend that *how* you show up is just as important. A key to being prepared and showing that you're ready is in being punctual. It is vital to success. To some people, being punctual is not a priority. It should be. If it hasn't been for you, I'd like to invite you to think again. There are many things that your punctuality, or lack thereof, communicates to yourself and to others.

Punctuality is the mark of a person who is self-disciplined. Being on time builds your self-confidence. It assures you can deliver your best. It demonstrates your attention to details. On a personal and professional level, being punctual shows you respect others. It's a promise you keep with yourself too. And honestly, it relieves you of the stress of lateness. Punctuality can truly affect your money. Take note. Early in my career I learned a valuable lesson about punctuality and how profitable punctuality can be. Check this out.

Runway Story Time—Sometimes Late Is Never

It pays to be on time. You may have heard the saying "Better late than never." Sometimes late *is* never. Few people know this, but in the movie *The Best Man,* there were supposed to have been four dancers, in addition to Candy, for the scenes I was in. Three of us showed up on time. One young lady showed up about two hours late. That is literally death to a movie set. Everything is on a schedule, and everything revolves around time on set. It doesn't matter if it is "hurry up and wait." This was also Malcolm Lee's film debut, so when the young lady finally arrived, he said, "Thank you for coming, but we no longer need your services."

When you are late, you slow down production. When you are late, you don't really know what opportunities are in front of you or what you may be missing out on. I had no idea, but in doing this film, I automatically became a part of the Screen Actors Guild (SAG) because I had a line in the movie. SAG is the union for actors. When you are in SAG, as part of the benefits you get protection for your residual income and on-set fees for hair and costume. Membership allows you to get paid fairly for your time, unlike how some non-union actors can be paid.

Follow me on this. I was completely unaware of how big the opportunity was that I was walking into. Six or seven years later, I realized exactly what had occurred. My mom forwarded mail sent to her because the Screen Actors Guild did not have my current address. The letter said that I had a trust set up for me at SAG. What?! I didn't know what they were talking about. When I investigated it further, I found out that because I was in SAG when I did *The Best Man,* I had accrued tens of thousands of dollars in residual income that I knew nothing about. I'm still earning from that movie years later, and will for a lifetime. Thank God I was on time!

Imagine if I had been late. Mic drop! Need I say more? I always share this story in my "Life of a Working Model Boot Camp" workshops for models who wish to break into or broaden their career in this industry that I love so much. You don't know what's ahead of you. It pays to be prepared. It pays, literally, to be punctual.

Let's go deeper on how punctuality profits you.

Being Punctual Builds Your Self-Confidence

Being on time reinforces your own belief in yourself. It builds your confidence because it shows you honor your commitments to yourself. Being punctual shows you're not willing to slack on yourself. You are willing do your best. Your value your own time. That alone causes your confidence to grow.

Punctuality Assures You Can Deliver Your Best

Have you ever shown up late for an appointment and had to rush? Your heart is racing. Your adrenaline is peaking. Sweat starts to pour from you. You keep glancing at your watch and feeling more and more anxious as you try to come up with an acceptable reason for why you're late. This is not good.

You arrived late, and now you're trying to get set up, only to find out that you left components at home or at the office that you needed. You were hurried and harried and simply bombed the presentation or speech. You were not on your game, perhaps because you lacked the timeliness to properly prepare yourself for success.

Contrast that with a time when everything was planned beforehand. You checked everything before you left. You arrived early enough to settle yourself, set up, and take a few breaths. You were calm, cool, and collected and ready to deliver. You could offer your best to whomever you were there to meet with or serve. Being on time assures that you can be on the top of your game. It allows you to confidently deliver your best. Don't others deserve to receive the very best of you? I'd say, "Yes!"

Being Punctual Shows You Respect Others

Perhaps you have not thought of this if you are chronically late. Not only does your lateness often

41

communicate an overall lack of professionalism but it shows a disregard for the time of others. Ouch! It may not be how you feel, but it can be how others perceive you. Your tardiness says that your time is more valuable than theirs. Have you ever considered that? People can miss opportunities when they are late because of how others feel disrespected by their lack of punctuality. They may then choose to not interact or work with you. No one wants to willingly work with someone who disrespects them. Be honorable. Be respectful. Be on time.

Being Punctual Relieves You of the Stress of Being Late

Punctuality is so important, not just in your career but in your life. Being late is stressful! There's something to be said about the calming effect of being on time. I used to be the person at the airport running to the gate, just barely getting on the plane before the doors closed. One day, the light came on. I had a conversation with myself, which is often where much greatness comes forth. I asked, "Why am I doing this to myself? It's so unnecessary!"

Now, don't get me wrong. I don't need to be super early, but I will not be late any more. I have chosen to be on time because it saves my own sanity. Running late fatigues you. You have to overcompensate for your tardiness, and it causes such mental and physical stress.

You might have to cut corners to push through things. It's just not worth it. You pay a bigger price than you realize. Timeliness allows me to be in the moment, and so I can shine. Don't miss your divine connection by not being on time. Lastly, is it possible that opportunities seemingly show up late for you because you're always late? Hmmm. Just a thought.

> *"Time is resource that you cannot get back.*
> *Respect it. Use it wisely."*
> *– Karin Haysbert*

The Successful Respect Time

Your time is one of your greatest resources. I don't know any great, powerful, and influential leaders operating at the highest level in their circles of influence who are haphazard about their time. Time is resource that you cannot get back. The successful know this. We understand that our profitability is in our making the most of it, and it starts with timeliness. It pays to be punctual in many ways. Greater peace. Greater ease. It allows you to perform at your best. It gives you the image of professionalism because you are ready. In short, it builds confidence. The most successful people are usually very conscious of their time and honor the time of others. Be on time.

Runway Story Time—Being Early Is On Time

Let's take it a step further. You may not know this, but I am a "footballnista." I love football! I have watched the game for years and attended more games than I can remember. New York Giants football fans (of which I am one, being from New York), and fans everywhere for that matter, remember the era of Coach Tom Coughlin. Coach Coughlin was notorious for being a stickler for punctuality. If you arrived at the meeting five minutes early, you were on time. If you arrived at the meeting at the scheduled time, my friend, you were late. Initially, this caused a big problem with his players, especially the veteran players, including one of the stars of the team, Michael Strahan.

Coughlin was merely trying to teach them lessons of discipline, hard work, and determination. Eventually, the message got through. When they realized that Coughlin really cared about them and only wanted to create winning attitudes in them, the angst between him and many of his team members became affection. They went on to win two Super Bowls against the vaunted New England Patriots. I saw a recent interview with Michael Strahan, and one of the things he said was that because of his experience with Coach Coughlin, his watch is still always set five minutes early. Now that's a lasting lesson. Punctuality matters!

Once you have mastered being on time, make every attempt to be early. Plan to be arrive a little earlier wherever you go. Map out your course. Check your route. Determine how much time it will take for you to get wherever you need to go, and then add an extra fifteen minutes. Punctuality is essential to your peaceful journey to success.

Runway Action Plan—Ask Yourself...

Grab your journal. Let's be honest.

How are you with time?

— Is time your friend?

— Are you missing opportunities, lucrative opportunities, because you have not disciplined yourself to be on time?

— Has your lateness alienated you from others? Damaged relationships?

— Can you identify the potential clients and cash you have lost because you have neglected punctuality?

— What adjustments do you need to make, if any, to improve your relationship with time and to be punctual?

"Practice isn't the thing you do once you're good.
It's the thing you do that makes you good."
– Malcolm Gladwell

45

"Practice creates confidence.
Confidence empowers you."
– Simone Biles

"I will be the first to say, when I started, I was the
worst on the runway ever. I feel like I try to keep
learning every time I step off a runway;
I try to get better with each one."
– Gigi Hadid

PRACTICE, PRACTICE, PRACTICE!

Practice is the repeated exercise for the purpose of gaining greater skill or proficiency. It empowers you to focus on what you want to improve and to achieve mastery. Successful people strive for excellence. Excellence can only be reached through practice. We've all heard that practice makes perfect. Even if it doesn't lead to perfection, practice certainly leads to progress, and progress is always beneficial. Whatever takes you forward is allowing you to get closer to your dreams of success.

Talent is never enough. I'll take a person who is moderately talented but committed to excellence over an exceedingly talented person who is indifferent about cultivating their greatness. Being committed to excellence develops character and allows you to be your best. Practice also create a level of confidence, so continued practice is an essential tool in your success toolbox. I have always said,

"You're never too good to get better."
– Liris

Why Practice Matters

Practice really is far reaching. No matter what level of proficiency you are at, you are never too good to get better. Practice develops you internally and externally. It builds your character and your competency.

If practice is so important, why do people skip practicing? Practice can be monotonous. It can be boring. It feels like nothing is happening sometimes. Practice will call on your deepest resources of faith during those times. It is in the valley of seeming non-movement that the consistency of practice strengthens you and sharpens your skills. It is often when we feel like no progress is being made that we then make a quantum leap in our development simply because we have been committed to practicing. This not only enlarges our inner being, but it cultivates our confidence too.

"Every hallway is a runway."
– Tyra Banks

Practice Is Your Confidence Booster

Practice pumps up your confidence. I believe we can always get better. I don't care how long I've been in this industry, there's always room for improvement. Even when I'm preparing for a runway show, I'll practice on the side of the stage. I practice at home. I can truly identify with Tyra Banks in finding a runway in every hallway—I practice in hallways too. I have a game plan. I already know when I hit the runway where I'll place my hands. I plan and practice my poses in advance and where I'll strike the poses. Of course, I flow in the moment also, but it gives me a sense of peace to practice and envision it beforehand. It allows me to go out and put my best foot forward on the runway because I have already practiced it before I hit the stage. I have already seen which aspects of the garment I will bring to life.

Let's go back to the saying that "practice makes perfect." When you feel you have reached a certain level of perfection beforehand, it gives you the confident feeling of "Hey, I got this!" Confidence raised.

Runway Story Time—Time to Make History

When I auditioned for my first job with *Project Runway* during season 14, I remember walking into the casting seeing models that I knew, models who were with agencies, models who were newbies in the game, and some who had been around for a while. I came in on a mission. I was not there to sit around and chat and chuckle. I came there to get this job. Another point— always walk in devout professionalism. I knew I could talk with them after I had fulfilled my purpose for the day.

I took the time to make sure I was in the right mind-set, because I wanted the opportunity so badly. While other girls were chumming it up, I went off to the side and practiced what I was going to do during my runway audition. I remember when I stepped down, one of the other models came up to me and said, "Liris, what are you over there practicing for? You know that you've got this."

That was a kind gesture, but I don't take anything for granted. I still go out there after over a decade in this industry and I practice, practice, practice. I practice like I did when I first started. I practice so that I can get into my rhythm. Your rhythm, in life and even in love, is important. Get into your flow. Find what feels good for you. You are never too good to get better. You can always grow.

Thankfully, I did end up booking the job with *Project Runway* during season 14 with the winning designer, Ashley Nell Tipton. I was the first black plus-size model to walk in a designer finale runway show. I'm honored and grateful for that. I prepared myself and practiced for it.

Runway Action Plan—Ask Yourself...

You know the routine. Grab your journal, and get ready to write.

What areas in your life could use some additional practice? How can you sharpen your skills and make yourself more valuable in your job, in your business, and in the work you do in the world? Are you practicing how you will give the presentation at work in your mirror at home? Do you practice what you will say at the networking event to assuage your jitters about connecting with strangers?

How about in your relationships? Do you practice improving how you communicate with your family member whom you may have had strained talks with? Do you need to practice how to speak kindlier? Could you practice at listening more acutely?

Where can you up-level your life and your confidence through greater practice? What are ways you can incorporate practice into your routine to give you a sense of belief and confidence in how you show up?

Practice! It strengthens your skills and boosts your confidence in the process.

"You can have all the potential in the world, but unless you have confidence, you have nothing."
– Tyra Banks

Talent Is Never Enough

Talent is certainly important. I do believe we all have natural, God-given giftings. However, what separates the good from the great is what we are willing to do with the talents we have been given. Are you willing to enhance your talents? Are you willing to sacrifice to make them their best? Will you put in the time and practice to allow their fullest expression?

Practicing takes character and increases it. It requires a level of self-discipline that people satisfied with mediocrity will not dedicate themselves to. Practice is hard work because it can be tedious. It's repetitious. It can get tiresome doing the same things over and over again. The road to success is paved with things others who are not as dedicated won't do. It's the things we do when others are sleeping or chilling. It's part of the price we pay in order to be great. You will constantly have to work on yourself to confidently live at that level.

Make a commitment to practice. Practice leads you to progress. It moves you forward. Practice until you are proficient. Reach your own level of excellence. Practice to your perfection. You can only be your very best at all times. Just practice. Take note of your progress, and celebrate your accomplishments.

"Live as if you were to die tomorrow. Learn as if you were to live forever."
– Ghandi

*"The journey is never ending. There's always
gonna be growth, improvement, adversity; you just
gotta take it all in and do what's right, continue to
grow, continue to live in the moment."*
— Antonio Brown

*"Personal development is the belief
that you are worth the effort, time, and energy
needed to develop yourself."*
— Denis Waitley

MASTER YOUR PERSONAL DEVELOPMENT— SPIRIT, SOUL, AND BODY

Personal development is an essential element to living in confidence and achieving success in life. It is the process by which you examine your life, take account of your strengths and weaknesses, skills and talents, and determine the goals necessary to reach your potential. It is a lifelong journey. When you know you are committed to constantly learning and growing, it builds confidence.

I personally read many books throughout the year. There is so much negative input that affects us throughout our lives, I counteract that by reading inspiring books and articles every day. I also daily watch videos that build me up, whether it is through YouTube or Periscope or some other livestream platform, as well as listen to podcasts.

Confidence comes from you esteeming yourself, but thankfully, there are many people throughout the world, like myself, who will encourage and motivate you as well. And when you don't have any confidence, you can borrow some of mine! That's what makes the world a great place. I think of it like we are all cups—if we keep pouring into each other, giving and receiving, we will never run dry.

We are here to help each other, to learn from each other, and to share in one another's growth. So please note—when you are having a bad day, don't sit in it alone for long. Call a loved one to support you. If you think there's no one to call right now, go online and get a little love from me or someone there. I think that's the good purpose of the internet—to share love and inspiration.

WALK IN THE SPIRIT

How's your relationship with God? Even if you don't believe in the same way I do, how can you tap into the power of love that is available to us all? This is vital to my success. I believe that once you develop that, your spiritual walk, it changes everything about your life.

My relationship with God sustains my whole life. It's amazing when you know who you are and whose you are because you operate from a different place. As I deepen my relationship with God, the things that would have made me distraught in the past almost seem meaningless. It has changed my entire focus. Truth be told, this relationship is the cornerstone of my confidence and success. Nothing else even comes close.

Because I know that God loves me and holds me in the highest esteem, I can hold myself there too. Recently I had a great friend of mine, albeit well meaning, try to tell me that some of my goals would happen down the road in five or ten years. Something in me confidently rose up and said, "Oh no, that's happening this year." That could only come from an assurance based on my closeness with my Creator. I have built myself up so spiritually and emotionally that I don't let anything anyone else says affect me much. When you are led from within, you are always on the right path.

*"Prayer is the key of the morning
and the bolt of the evening."*
– Ghandi

*"God is ever present. He's in every breath, in every
step. He's here, always, always."*
– Jill Scott

"Pray without ceasing."
– 1 Thessalonians 5:17

THE SECRET TO MY SUCCESS

Do you want to know the secret to my success? It's prayer. Before I go out on any runway or walk before any cameras on a photo shoot, I always pause. I take a moment. I give thanks for the opportunity to share my gifts. I pray for the wisdom, creativity, and ingenuity to let my light shine. It is the key to my success. It can be the way to your success too. There is a perfect plan for you to manifest your best life. Why not ask? Get still. Get quiet so you can hear what would give you the favor, protection, and provision to bring forth success in your life.

The Power of Prayer

Let's talk about the power of prayer. Prayer is a potent part of your spiritual growth no matter what your personal beliefs are. Prayer is dialogue, that is, two-way communication. It's not just talking to God, but it is also listening. As you may know, vibrant, healthy communication is the lifeblood of any relationship we have, whether it is business or personal. There's a sensitivity that I gain through prayer where I know in my heart just what to do. This gives me a peace that cannot come from any other source. Consistent prayer can help you release your burdens, so you can know you will be okay. You have been heard, felt, and understood. When I earnestly pray, I know that I can drop my concerns off and keep it moving.

It's important for me to keep God at the center of life through prayer, no matter what. Prayer is also that connection that we can tap into to empower us when we don't feel like going on. When we practice prayer and do our work, it takes us to a whole new level, a level of divine truth. It paves the way for our dreams to manifest. Most of all, prayer facilitates the ultimate relationship. We feel safe, and we know that eventually, no matter how difficult life becomes, all things will work out for our good.

Your Power Source

Let's face it. Sometimes, life can just suck. Nothing seems to be going your way. Everything you try seems to fail. Have you ever felt like "Why bother? I give up!"? I have many times. I have felt powerless, like nothing seems to be working. I actually felt like this last year before the awesome opportunity to be on *Project Runway* fell into my lap. I was mentally and physically drained because the year started terribly, and nothing was working right. We've all gone through those difficult seasons. That's when I know I'm not connected. It's like unplugging your TV and wondering why you can't see the picture on the screen. I plug in through prayer. It's my power source. Through prayer you can begin to feel that help is coming. You will be reminded of how great you really are and that your situation is turning in your favor.

The Ultimate Reset

Prayer is the ultimate reset for me. It reminds me that every day is a new day. It is a new opportunity to get it right. We can reset our lives through saying our prayers and casting our cares. Prayer strengthens me to let go of the things that are behind me. It's a total attitude adjustment. When God says to let go, who am I to argue with Him? I know He knows what's best for me. It's in prayer that I am restored so I can move forward powerfully.

It reminds me of when your phone gets stuck in a program. It won't move forward. It won't allow you to do anything else. You have to cut it off and back on so that it can reset itself. That's what prayer does for me. It cuts me off from the problems and stresses of life and cuts me on to love. In prayer, I get unstuck. I discover the answers to life's questions that perplex me. I know that I am plugging in to love, and that always points me in the right direction for my life.

Surrender

Prayer calls me to surrender. We often view surrendering as giving up. That could be seen as a sign of weakness, but *to surrender* actually shows profound strength and trust. I need to surrender when I'm holding on to people or circumstances too tightly. I need to surrender when my mind is needlessly wrapped up in the futility of worrying. I need to surrender when fear is trying to break my heart and snuff out my hope. Prayer reminds me to surrender to God because I know that I'm never alone. Just like the image of someone walking out with their hands lifted surrendering, that is what I do in prayer. I lift my hands, I take my hands off things, and I let go and let God.

Here are a few thoughts on deeper surrender that came up from me just a couple weeks ago, which I shared on social media. I regularly share Liris Motivates posts. You can follow me on Facebook and Instagram @lirisc:

> The word "surrender" popped into my head. That's actually the flow of my life lately. I have surrendered my life to God's plan and all the possibilities it brings. I don't allow anxiety or worry to overcome me. I flow in ease. My schedule has been bonkers lately with things that could send me into a tailspin. How am I going to work this out? How am I going to make this or that happen? I've simply replied to my agents and friends that "God is in control and everything will work out for my good" and it has. I just keep on doing my part. Have faith or worry, but you can't do both. Plus, worry is a waste of time and energy, so surrender. God's got You. Trust. I'm a witness.
>
> Liris

I Belong

I belong to God. When I contemplate that I am a child of God, and I know that I am God's best because I am fearfully and wonderfully made, it allows me to walk in a higher level of confidence. You can too! When you know that you belong to God, the stuff that would defeat you in the past has no effect on you. Belonging makes you sure-footed. That's why my relationship with God is so important and why I tap into Him. The world may say one thing, but if I know that God said another to me, it leads me to believe differently. It gives me a new level of confidence. My self-worth soars. Here's a truth: You cannot go or stay anywhere that you do not feel you belong, whether it is in the boardroom with a seat at the table or sharing your life with an amazing partner. Know that you belong and that you have a right to a blessed life. Catch that!

KNOW WHO YOU ARE

What a lot of people are missing regarding their confidence is that they don't know who they are. When you know you are God's creation, you realize you aren't junk. It doesn't matter if you are super skinny or super heavy or what society deems as beautiful or not. He made you, and you are beautiful in His eyes. You're here for purpose. You're here because you are necessary. Everybody has their preferences, and it really doesn't matter what others say or believe. As the saying goes, "One man's trash is another man's treasure." We are all treasure, and that is what matters most.

I'm Just Like You

I'm just like you. Many people look at me or others like me and assume that because we have money or power or great looks that everything in our lives goes perfectly. They conclude that we don't go through trials and tribulations or experience moments of low self-esteem. That's not true. People are people, whether poor or rich, handicapped or not, red, black, brown, yellow, or white. We all share in the same human experience.

Please don't think that because I am a supermodel and have a nice shape and a beautiful face that I have never thought about ending my own life. I have thought about it, but thankfully, I didn't. God sent certain people into my life to help hold me together. I also leaned on Him at my lowest points and had to remember who I am in Him. That was the game changer. I'm glad I overcame and lived my life, because that's why I'm still here today and able to write this book to speak life into you, so you can make the world your runway. It's my purpose to give you confidence and a new way of looking at yourself. If you're reading this, you have so much more to give to the world—so many ideas, so much love, so much time, so much beauty. I hope that you understand how important your love and confidence in yourself is to your purpose. I pray that you grasp how much your purpose means to the world so that you can be your best and live fearlessly.

Runway Story Time

When I say I am just like you, I mean it. Life is interesting. People will say things to me or about me, and I honestly feel like, "Whatever!" Recently on social media, a troll said some very negative and hurtful things about me on my channel. I don't usually address them; I just block them. But this time I did confront him, and used it as a teaching opportunity.

My sentiment was that no matter what anyone says, I'm still getting paid. I'm still cute. I'm still highly desired. I'm still fabulous. I'm still a great aunt. I'm still a great sister. I'm still a great daughter. I'm still a great public speaker. I'm still a top model. God loves me. I love myself and so do a lot of other people too. So, your point?

It was literally like water on a duck's back. It rolled right off. I shared it, and people were so angry that someone would say anything like that to me or about me. They were hurt for me. One of my girlfriends was literally crying about it. She was so upset. I told her that she didn't need to feel badly because I don't feel badly about it.

Periodically, I share those experiences on social media with others because many times people think I have everything in life and that everything is perfect in my life. They think that because I have an hourglass shape or curvy body, I am the desire of every man. They think no one talks down to me or about me. They think I don't understand what it is to go through what they go through.

That's not true. I am you. We share the same joys and sorrows. No matter how perfect you think someone's body or life is, other people think differently. So what. Opinions are like noses. Everybody has one. I wanted them to see that I get the same attacks from time to time too, but I calmly put them in their place and keep it moving.

Sometimes the best response is no response at all. Refuse to justify their very existence in that negative place. You have to be so sure of who you are that what anyone else thinks you are is of no consequence. That's a choice you make.

The me that I am today has grown over time because I lean in to God and believe His voice of love toward me. Who cares about the haters with a love surrounding me that strong? It drowns out the haters.

Runway Action Plan—Ask Yourself...

Grab your journal. Let's investigate your spiritual life.

— How will you develop a stronger spiritual walk?

— How will you get quiet so you can hear God's or Spirit's voice?

— When will you set aside time daily to pray?

— What prayer requests do you have for each area of your life?

— What is the outcome you desire? (Please note: always leave room for God to amaze you.)

— How can you make your life a prayer?

Do Your Soul Work

Know that you are worth it! I love that quote by Denis Waitley: "Personal development is the belief that you are worth the effort, time, and energy needed to develop yourself." I'm worth the effort. The time and money I spend investing in my own development is time and money well spent. You are your greatest asset. If I told you that I had a rare, one-of-a-kind, precious gem the world had never seen before, which had unparalleled worth, and told you that you could have access to it, would you be interested?

You already do. That precious gem is you! Your growth and evolution are priceless. As similar as we are, there is no one in the world exactly like you. When God made you, He broke the mold. You were sent here with skills that only you have, because they can only be presented in the way you can offer them. You aren't just a one in a million. You are the ONLY ONE!

When you consider that, who can compete with you? Who can surpass you when you are being authentically you and work to be your very best? No one can. You are worth the effort of working on yourself. You deserve to be your best. We need the gifts that only you can give. Receive that deep within.

INVEST IN YOURSELF

Considering the enormous gift that you are, understand that it comes in seed form. You have the capacity to be great in every way, but it's like a seed that must be nurtured in order to grow. Are you willing to invest in yourself? Every time I speak at women's conferences, industry events, youth events, or even for the Model Boot Camps that I offer, I always invite others to invest in themselves. You're worth it.

There are so many tools today to assist you in that. This book is one of them. Take the time to work on yourself and put your money where your mouth is. Invest money in conferences, workshops, and classes. Take online courses. Invest in things to expand your craft. Hire a coach or a mentor. Join groups with like-minded people who want to grow in a way that you are working on. It's all about you becoming your best you. One thing is constant. Change is inevitable. Since I'm going to change, I want to be purposeful about my changing for the better. Invest in yourself. You are worth the investment. If you are interested in building greater poise, power, profitability, and success on the runway and off, go to www.LirisC.com for more information about my workshops.

"Sometimes we want our lives to go where our minds have never been."
– Apostle Kenneth O. Robinson

SAMPLE SUCCESS

Why do we want our lives to go where our minds have never been? If we want our lives to go anywhere, we must go there within first. One of the easiest ways to do that is to sample your success. It helps to condition your mind into believing that you belong there. It's yours. You will never be where you don't feel like you belong. Or if you do get there, you won't stay there. That's why most lottery winners are flat broke within a couple of years. They didn't feel that they really belonged there.

I don't want that to happen to you. Sample your success. Visualize it, but go and experience it for yourself. It might be staying at a fancy hotel just for the night. You may even go to a five-star restaurant and just order dessert and coffee. Take a tour of a country club. Visit an exotic car lot and go for a test drive. Splurge on a VIP or luxury experience. Go to the most exquisite boutique and simply try the clothing on. In the dressing room, take pictures of yourself in them. Feel the quality of the clothes. Allow these things to become familiar to you. Whatever success would look or feel like to you, go sample it. This will help to acclimate your mind and heart to receive it.

Develop Your Body Temple

Although it is vitally important to develop yourself spiritually, emotionally, and intellectually, it is equally important to develop your physical body. As far as I know, you only get one body. Developing it to be healthy and strong should be very close to the top of your list of priorities. Does it matter how spiritually evolved you are if you drop dead the next day because you totally ignored the temple in which you reside?

Although we are in a time where everyone wants to be accepted as they are, and I agree with that, I also believe that our acceptance of ourselves should come with a healthy enough love for ourselves to do what's best for us. With that being said, I must address the concern I have.

There are some curves that are not healthy, just like there are some people who are underweight and unhealthy. Both can be hazardous to one's health. Yes, I said it. It does not mean that you love yourself any less. I believe that you love yourself enough to be proactive about getting yourself in the healthiest state possible. Everyone has a weight in which their body can function at its best. Weight is not the only measure of health, but it is one of them. I've said numerous times in interviews that being plus size doesn't automatically make you unhealthy, just like being skinny doesn't automatically make you healthy. If you are struggling to walk a block or climb a flight of stairs, are unable to do anything in your normal life because you cannot carry the weight you have on your frame, or are too weak because of the weight you don't have, with love, it's time to do something about that. Let me say it again. I believe in healthy curves no matter the size of those curves. This goes both ways.

Please, let's not fool ourselves into believing that your size doesn't matter when it comes to your health. It does. While I have seen or read about people who seem to have been the picture of health die unexpectedly from a heart attack or develop a grave disease, there may be other factors that led to that. Let's not use that as an excuse to not take control and responsibility of our own physical development and health.

Move Your Body!

Get moving! Go for a walk or hike. Hit a bike trail. Work out in a fitness class. Try Zumba or spin class. Go sweat in a hot yoga studio. Play basketball with friends for an hour. Join a softball or volleyball league. You know you still have some of those skills from high school. Go bowling. Be a part of a team. Truth is, you learn so much from team activities. It promotes growth in you. And competition can build character while being fun too.

Whatever strikes your fancy, get up and get moving. Years ago, the NFL unveiled an initiative called "Play

60," encouraging young people to make a commitment to a healthier lifestyle by going out to move and play for sixty minutes a day. I love that! You might not have sixty minutes, but can you give yourself thirty minutes? Even fifteen minutes beats none.

You are here for a very special purpose, and you deserve to live this life with a sense of health, vitality, and energy. Actually, you need that in order to live out your purpose on the Earth. Let's be responsible. Take your physical development as seriously as every other area of your life.

RAISE YOUR STANDARDS

Now here's the truth. You will never rise above the standards you set for yourself. My sister always says, "Standards are what you allow." What does that mean? You might say your standard is one thing, but if you allow something else, that's the real standard. I know that this is sometimes a hard pill to swallow, but I need you to take a big gulp of water and swallow it. Raise your standards. Refuse to tolerate any area of your life being below the standard of excellence that you desire. This applies to every area of your life. What you tolerate you will have. Refuse to tolerate the spiritual, mental, emotional, or physical habits that are not taking you where you want to go. Refuse to tolerate relationships that no longer serve you. Refuse to tolerate a workplace situation that is making you sick. Refuse to tolerate a victim mentality in yourself. Refuse to tolerate that excess weight that might be killing you. Refuse to tolerate people's constant lack of appreciation or mistreatment of you. Take a stand for yourself. Do something about it. Set high standards. Strengthen your spiritual walk. Elevate your mind-set. Create new habits. Review them, and work toward living to be your best self.

CELEBRATE YOUR SUCCESSES

This is an often-overlooked aspect of success. Not only does celebrating your successes cause you to become focused on what you are grateful for, but it allows you to really appreciate who you are and what you've done. When you celebrate your successes, no matter how large or small, you are telling yourself *achieving is a great thing* and *please give me more to celebrate.* Your mind is always looking for ways to prove yourself right. If you are always focused on the many accomplishments you have each day, your mind will help you to achieve more. If you reach your goal and don't reward yourself in any way, pretty soon your mind will say, "What's the use?" That is why you must be grateful each day. You must look for what went well. You must focus on how you won that day. Did you do your morning routine? Did you make it to the gym and get a great workout in? Did you return all the phone calls you had planned to? Did you make a point of spending quality time with your children? Did you take time to relax? Did you get that big client you've been going after? Whatever your wins for the day are, intentionally focus on them. How will you reward yourself every step of the way? I promise you this will increase your levels of confidence and success in life.

Runway Action Plan—Your Personal Development Course

Earlier in this chapter, we identified goals in various areas of your life. This is where the rubber must meet the road. It's time to put it into action. You've developed visions, now you must put them into practical steps.

— How do you eat an elephant? One bite at a time. Set big goals, but break them into smaller steps. Implement them one step at a time.

— Here's the next big question. Who do you have to become inside in order to achieve those goals?

— What are your strengths?

— What are your weaknesses?

— Which of each area matters most with regard to your purpose?

— What personal qualities must be established and matured in you?

— What character qualities do you need to develop to thrive in your relationships?

— What's the most important thing you can change about yourself to foster your career success?

— What can you work on to stimulate your creative genius?

— What would improve your relationship with money and finances?

— How do you need or desire to feel so that you can fully step up to the plate in life?

Your answers will determine what your personal development course must be. While it's important to identify where you want to go, it's equally imperative to clarify the person you will have to become in the process to reach those goals.

You know what's next. Grab your journal. I invite you to take some quiet time now to really think about who you are now. Consider who you must develop into so you can live out your dreams confidently. It is the only way that you will make the world your runway.

Be gut-level honest. If you know you have been lazy and must develop greater diligence in your work habits, tell the truth. If you realize you have been selfish and need to be more open to being available to your family to build closer relationships, say that too. You can do it! The journey to success is paved on the roads of personal development. Most of all, celebrate your successes. This ensures that they keep coming.

71

*"Self-love has very little to do with
how you feel about your outer self.
It's about accepting all of yourself."
— Tyra Banks*

*"It's all about falling in love with yourself
and sharing that love with someone who
appreciates you, rather than looking for love to
compensate for a self-love deficit."
— Eartha Kitt*

*"An empty lantern provides no light. Self-care is
the fuel that allows your light to shine brightly."
— Unknown*

SELF-LOVE AND SELF-CARE

Are You in Love with Yourself?

I believe that part of your personal development includes how you love and care for yourself. Do you love yourself? I mean, really. Do you? If you don't, that's your first step. I love Eartha Kitt's wise words above. You must fall in love with yourself first. How can you expect anyone else to fall in love with you when you aren't in love with yourself?

Once you love and accept yourself and are able to see the beauty in who you are, then you can fully share that love with others. You can attract people to appreciate you because you appreciate yourself. Mother Maya

Angelou taught us that we teach people how to treat us. We do that by the way we treat ourselves. Your search for love starts with you loving yourself. An outside person cannot fill a self-love deficit.

Think of your very best friend, the friend who loves and accepts you the most. How do they see you? What great things would they say about you? What about you brings them joy? Then, realize they have only scratched the surface. There is so much more to you that hasn't even yet been revealed. Trust that. Every day purposefully think of how you excel at things, what you are great at, and the quality of person you are. Compliment yourself to yourself. I promise you, this will change your whole identity. If you daily see goodness in yourself, your self-love and self-esteem will soar.

Self-Care Is NOT Selfish

I know the "self-care is not selfish" theme is a highly touted concept, but so few of us seem to live it out. You can change this if it's not true for you now. It's high time that you treated yourself! I will say it again, treat yourself! It's important that you have a personal care plan inside and outside. Pamper yourself. Take loving care of yourself. Get your eyebrows waxed. Indulge in a lavish massage and a relaxing facial. Beautify your hands and feet with a spa manicure and pedicure. Take a long, hot, bubble bath. Let's talk about baths for a moment. My sister told me about a cool acronym she heard for *bath* at a Women's Conference many years ago. It is this: BATH—**B**eing **A**ble **T**o **H**ear. There is something mystical that happens when you are in water.

I was on a job in Utah for Maggie Sottero the other day. When I arrived at the hotel after a long day's work, I put my phone on Do Not Disturb so I had no calls or texts to distract me, and I took a long, hot, bubble bath. That was self-love time just for me. I blocked everybody else out. I put on some soothing sounds from Myles Davis and just chilled in the tub for a whole hour.

I will add another acronym: BATH—**B**eing **A**ble **T**o **H**eal. In a bath, you get to submerge yourself in this body of water and perhaps some healing oils. It's almost like being in the womb. Something about it is healing. It gives you a chance to hear and to heal. It stands to reason that because our bodies are mostly made up of water, that going back into that element has to bring healing and wholeness. Take a bath!

Take Loving Care

Lovingly care for yourself. Go for a walk on a beautiful trail. Sit by a stream. Take a journal and visit a state park, pack a picnic lunch, and just camp out for half a day all alone. Binge watch one of your favorite shows and laugh until you cry. Read a mystery novel. Say no to an event you feel too tired to attend so you can go to bed early. Say yes to something you have put off but always wanted to do. Sit in silence for as long as you want to.

Yell. Scream. Punch pillows until any anger leaves you. Go help someone else in need.

I don't know what makes you feel loved and cared for, but you should. If you don't, now is the time to think intently about it, to try new things until you find what works for you. Too often, we deny ourselves the pleasures of life. Why? You only live once. You might as well enjoy yourself.

I have found that as I intentionally do what expresses self-love and self-care for myself, these practices help to bring peace to my life. They will do the same for you. A confident woman or man is peaceful. She or he is not worried and worn out. Put yourself at the top of your list again or for the first time, but do it. Will you commit to that now? Even if you have to start small, start.

Tap into Your Inner Child

There is so much joy that can be derived from tapping into your inner child. The truth is that you were born confident. The experiences of life talked you out of your confidence. You had no self-esteem issues as a baby. Babies completely love and enjoy every part of themselves from their bald heads to their tasty toes. Every now and then, I tap into my inner child, and what she loved and enjoyed, and honor it. It's a part of my self-love and self-care.

Growing up, my mom sent me to dance class. I took modern dance and ballet. I can't move today like I did back then, but I still love to dance. I love music. Most of the time I'm either listening to Periscope or listening to music. It feels loving to me to be able to move and dance to beautiful music in a room. That's something that my inner child enjoyed and still enjoys today. To me, it's freeing. It allows me to communicate with my body in a way that brings me joy. I ask you. What does that for you?

Runway Story Time

I have lived with the pain and discomfort of having a herniated disc in my back for years. As a model, I spend numerous hours on my feet. It can be as many as sixteen-hour days in high heels, contorting my body into poses. Whoever thought modeling was easy has never modeled!

Recently, I received a penetrating, deep-tissue massage. When I left there, I had the most glorious attitude. I felt invigorated. Even when I woke up the next morning, I felt so refreshed in my mind, body, and spirit that working out didn't seem like a hardship. Yes, I advocate for healthy curves and have to push myself to exercise sometimes too, LOL. I felt completely rejuvenated. My back was not hurting, so I didn't have that excuse to hold me back from getting my workout in.

Since I had taken care of myself, it gave me a fresh wind. Offering my physical body what it needed allowed me to be more agile and moldable. It empowers me to bring the right energy to the runway and perfected poses to my shoots that stretch beyond what I am normally capable of doing had I not attended to my own physical self-care. Take care of yourself.

Runway Action Plan: Your Personal Self-Love & Self-Care Plan

Grab your journal. It's time to write.

Take a few moments right now and write thirty things that would make you feel happy or that you know would make you feel great after you do them. I say things *you know would make you feel better afterwards* too, because sometimes there are things that don't necessarily seem so great, like exercise. However, the benefits and how wonderful you feel afterwards far outweigh the slight discomfort of getting started.

SIDE NOTE. *Speaking of exercise, it is one of the quickest ways I know of to change how you feel. If you're feeling down, go to a Zumba class to get the blood pumping, ride a bike trail, go to a dance party to tear it up, or hit the sidewalk for a brisk walk. The movement changes your state, releases endorphins in your body, and causes you to de-stress and feel better. Now that's self-love and self-care.*

After you've made this list, choose one to two of these items to do every single day. If you don't take care of yourself, who will? You show others how to treat you by the way you treat yourself.

WELCOME CONSTRUCTIVE CRITICISM

Welcome criticism? Yes. Constructive criticism is necessary for your full development. If you are a person who is touchy about anyone giving you any feedback, you're in trouble. You have to accept that you have blind spots. There are things you do that you are completely unaware of. Confident, self-assured people welcome feedback and constructive criticism from others around them because we always want to be our best. We know we don't know or see everything about ourselves. We're willing to hear others out and to consider if we need to shift. We will talk more about relationships later, but put this in your heart and practice it in your life.

"Four steps to achievement: Plan purposefully. Prepare prayerfully. Proceed positively. Pursue persistently."
– William A. Ward

"I love the confidence that makeup gives me."
– Tyra Banks

"Just because you can wear a micro-mini skirt, it doesn't mean you should." – Cindy Crawford

"When you look good, you feel good. Confidence with what you're wearing is very important. If you feel good, you will always perform your best without worrying about anything."
– Maria Sharapova

– 3 –

PRESENTATION POWER

YOUR PRESENTATION IS YOUR OFFERING to the world. It is the message you want to convey. It's the feeling you want to give to others about yourself. There is a passage in the Bible that says, "Man looks at the outward appearance, but God looks at the heart." Remember that. Only God, and maybe your mama, just looks at your heart. Let's face it, in order to walk in runway confidence, you have to pay attention to how your outer and inner appearances are. Take care of how you present yourself.

I think we live in a world today that screams from the mountaintops about how they don't care what anybody thinks of them, when secretly, they really do. Further, they should. While I am certainly not suggesting we care about what others think of us to hold us in bondage to their opinions, it is important that we present ourselves in a way that our contribution can be received. Besides, you live in a world with other people, not just God or your mama. Let's talk about packaging yourself in the most favorable way.

When I meet a client for the first time, I do my research. I see what their models look like. I look at the types of products they sell. I make sure I dress like their brand with my own personal flair added to it. I look like I belong with their company. I firmly believe my planning and preparation leads to me giving a proper presentation to them. Do you look like the role or position you are in? Do you look like the position you desire?

"You never get a second chance
to make a first impression."
– Will Rogers

FIRST IMPRESSIONS ARE LASTING

Within just a few seconds of meeting or interacting with others, you have made a lasting impression about who you are to them. First impressions are lasting. Look the part. Today, we talk quite a bit about the dangers of judging others. I understand that, but it is completely normal for everyone to create at least an initial opinion about you right away. Because of that, we must be very attentive to how we are presenting of ourselves.

What impression are you making? Now, I'm going to give a little tough love here, and you may feel like this is common sense, but as my sister, Karin, says, "Sense ain't common or else everybody would use it." We've talked a bit about taking care of yourself, and these things are important to your overall presentation. Ladies, ladies, ladies—get your nails done. Not only does it feel good to have your hands and feet taken care of, but it adds to your overall polished presentation. Brothers, you too. Real talk. We don't need your old, scraggly feet cutting us up in bed. Go get those heels shaved down. We use our hands when we talk. We touch people with our hands. Use scrubs and lotions so that your hands are soft and smooth. Guys, remove those calluses from your hands.

PULL YOURSELF TOGETHER!

Remember, your presentation is crucial whether you are going to a job interview or out on that first date. How you present yourself feeds into others' perception of you. If your nails look a mess, your shoes are scuffed and dirty, or your hair looks unkempt, it will probably lead people to get a negative impression of you. They will never get to experience the wonder of who you are. I know we want to say you shouldn't judge a book by its cover, but people do it all the time—including you. Pull yourself together so you can truly make the world your runway!

You Deserve to Look Good and to Feel Good

You deserve to look good. When you look good, it helps you to feel good. You deserve to treat yourself in this way. You deserve to be perceived as someone who cares about themselves enough to take care of themselves. It is a way that you show yourself care. Your maintenance makes the statement about you.

Evaluate how you feel about shaving. I personally get bikini waxes. I shave my legs. I shave my underarms. I get my eyebrows waxed. I get any hair, no matter how fine, off my upper lip. Because I model swimwear, I have even gotten laser hair removal around my bikini line. It's what I need to look my best for my jobs, so I go through the pain and discomfort to get it done. Why? Because I know that the outcome will be better. The presentation will be smoother, and so will I. All that matters. I don't want to do a bikini shoot that the photographer has to zoom in and retouch areas on the shots on my legs because of hair stubble, shaving bumps, or discolorations from shaving.

You Never Know...

Again, you never know who you're going to run into. You could be at the grocery store or at church and meet your future spouse. Yesss! Real Talk. Ladies, he should not see you with a bonnet on your head and wearing pajama bottoms. In public? Really? Brothers, we look at your hands and your shoes. If you have dirt under your fingernails, it's a real turnoff. What about your shoes? Are they dusty and mangled? How do your shoestrings look? Are they even clean? All of that gives others an impression of you. Take pride in yourself. Show that you care about yourself. People respect that.

YOU ARE ROYALTY

On *Project Runway* they called me Queen Liris. They saw me as a woman who is sure of who she is. I am confident in who I am. I carry myself like a queen. I am no different than you are. You can carry yourself like royalty every day. Walk, talk, and present yourself like the king or queen you are.

> *"No matter how you feel, get up,*
> *dress up and show up."*
> *– Regina Brett*

Runway Action Plan—Ask Yourself...

Grab your journal. Let's be real.

— How are you dressed?

— Is it appropriate for the occasion, or do you have the "I can wear whatever I want and y'all need to respect me anyway" attitude?

— Are your clothes ironed?

— Do you greet others with a warm smile?

— Are you friendly, courteous, and kind, or are you gossiping about everyone who passes by?

— Do you look like a confident person?

— Do people wonder who you are when you walk into a room?

You can't think for others, and you aren't responsible for how they feel, but you are responsible for how you represent yourself to them. Represent yourself well.

Dress How You Wish to Be Addressed

I know, I know. Please, dress how you wish to be addressed. I cannot stress this enough. I do not say this because I am in the fashion industry. I say this because it is true. You have complete control over your personal appearance. How you dress accounts for so much of what you say about yourself, at least initially. It affects how people perceive you and address you. If you wish to be addressed like a person of great position and power, you must look like a person of great position and power. You get to choose the tone for how you show up in the world, and it doesn't mean you have to have cookie-cutter style.

Dress for Your Next Level

Always dress for where you're going, not for where you are right now. Dress for your next level. There are so many options available today, even for plus-size women, at all price points. Strive to look like the confident, successful man or woman that you are or are in the making. It's better to have a few great pieces you look great in and that make you feel like a million bucks than to have a closet full of cheap, trendy things that will be out of style as soon as the season ends. Choose wisely.

BE HONEST ABOUT WHAT SIZE YOU ARE NOW

You can tell how serious someone is about their job or career just by how sharp and clean their clothing looks. Ladies, I say this with love. Please wear the right size. I know that it's your favorite suit, and you've gained just a little weight over the years, but if you no longer fit it well, retire it. This happens to us all. We've gone to a larger size and don't want to accept it, so we keep squeezing into the smaller size (looking and feeling like a stuffed sausage, mind you), saying that one day we'll lose that extra weight. Until you do, get some clothes that look great on you now, and put those other clothes aside. It is much better that you look and feel your best than to hold on to your former self and its wardrobe. Remember, people are addressing you by the appearance they see now. Let it be pristine. The more comfortable you are in good fitting clothes, the more confident you come across too.

The Plus-World Rebellion

This actually may step on toes. It's not my intention to hurt anyone's feelings. Just because something is made in your size, it does not mean that you should wear it. I feel like the plus world is in a bit of a rebellion. I think it stems from having muumuus be the acceptable option for so long and not having been properly catered to in the past. Because we haven't had the same style options as our straight-size sisters, now that some brands are stepping outside their boxes and making fashion options in all sizes, we are just putting it on whether it is high-cut bathing suits, certain types of bodycon dresses, or miniskirts.

Here's the thing. You are welcome to wear whatever you want to, but it doesn't mean that it's going to look great on you. I dress to show my body best. I'm not trying to prove a point. I'm not trying to make a cultural statement. I am trying to look my best and to feel my best.

Dress to Show Your Body Best

Sometimes people think that because I have an hourglass shape, I can wear anything. Not true! I may have an hourglass shape, but I also have broad shoulders and large breasts. I also do have a big butt. I know that there is a very fine line regarding what I can wear where I can look sexy and classy or trashy. I choose to dress sexy and classy, so I have to find things that adorn my shape and in the most flattering way.

There are certain cuts of skirts I cannot wear because it will make me look boxy or heavier than I really am. I like to look the size that I am. So I'm very aware of what styles look best on me. It really doesn't matter what's considered en vogue if it doesn't make me look fabulous.

Certain bathing suits don't make my body look great. When shopping for a bathing suit, consider whether you have a long torso or a short torso. Do you have long legs or short legs? Do you have broad shoulders and small breasts? Or do you have small shoulders and large breasts? Take all these things into consideration when you dress yourself. I've been on beaches and seen women from size 4 to size 28. I've seen women who were plus size who wore a suit that fit them well and looked better in their presentation than our smaller sisters. It's not about size. It's about finding flattering fits.

GET YOURSELF A TAILOR

Get yourself a skilled tailor. Sometimes you can find a gem of one at your local dry cleaners. This is not just for plus-size women. This is for all women. For our brothers, you should not be buying a suit off the rack and wearing it unless it fits you amazingly. Go get it tailored. Get it taken in so that it shows the cut of your body in the best possible way. This is for straight-sized men and women to plus-size men and women. Because of my body shape, I often have to get my jeans tailored and taken in at the waist. This is another moment where you must invest in yourself. Spend the few extra dollars so that you will look your very best.

Stop thinking that every clothing line is going to fit you. If you find something you absolutely love, but it's actually made for a different body shape, spend the money and get it altered so it can fit you perfectly. Because I am 5 feet, 11 inches, I may need to let a hem out or even bring it higher. I might want to close up a split in a skirt or dress or have it opened up and taken higher. It all depends on where it hits my body.

I have always loved the Gap. Their ads have intrigued me. The pictures in their stores have always appealed to me too, but whoever they use for their fit models must have a different shape than I do. As much as I love their jeans, they don't fit me. Every designer does not design for everybody. Fashion should be extremely personal to you. Make it work for you.

HAVE FUN WITH FASHION

Have fun with fashion. Even if it is not joyful for you now, intend to make fashion a pleasurable playground. Fashion is meant to be lived in with joy. Here's what I mean by that. I want you to experiment with it. Play with jewelry accessories, scarves, belts, hats, pins, and brooches. Even finding the right tailor to customize your garments so that they fit you like a glove can make fashion fun for you. You'd be surprised how much of a difference it makes and how great it feels when your clothing fits you perfectly.

Because I have broad shoulders, if I have a television interview, I have to be strategic. We all know television adds weight to your frame anyway. I try not to wear things that are cut on my arms because it will make me look really boxy, since the shot is usually like a headshot. I will wear a sleeve that at least goes to my elbows. Know what works best for your body.

TAKE YOURSELF IN

To know what's best for you, you have to take yourself in. How? Here's what I do. Go to your favorite department store. I personally love Macy's. Visit your favorite departments in the store and pull a lot of clothes. Try a variety of designers too. You will find that some fit well on you, while others do not. Make note of those that work.

Try different cuts of clothes. Do A-line skirts flatter you, or do pencil-cut skirts look best? Are you most comfortable with straight-leg, wide-leg, bootcut, mid-rise, or low-rise pants or jeans? Can you rock a bodycon dress, or would a wrap dress be more appealing on you? Does a peplum dress do it for you, or are you a maxi-dress girl? Have fun with it. Experiment with different styles and colors.

Ladies, wear whatever you want, but make sure that it works for YOU. I do want to address one thing here. There has been a sentiment that plus-size women cannot wear cropped tops. I disagree. I do think you need to consider how much you show and where your top is cropped. Ask yourself. Is it flattering to show that area on you? Not on anyone else, but on you? If it is, then by all means, show it. Little adjustments like this make all the difference. This goes back to knowing your body, taking yourself in, and knowing what is best and most complimentary for you.

Personally, I know that off the shoulder styles look great on me, especially if I can do something to bring in the waist to give beautiful balance to my look. Play around with different fashions. Fashion really is your friend. It's here to make you look good. It's all about finding what works for you. When you do, get in front of that mirror and take yourself in. Take it and run with it.

Runway Story Time

I'm going to share a story about a family member who has given me permission to share. I hope that you will get something from this. It's interesting, but my older sister, Karin, who I think is absolutely beautiful, has often struggled with feeling rather insecure and indifferent about fashion. When she grew up, she was very skinny and tall. She never seemed to be able to find things that fit her well. They were either too big in some areas or often too short because of her long legs and slim physique.

When I was talking with her about fashion being her friend, she sort of cringed. For most of her life she has had a feud, not a friendship, with fashion. I write this part of the book for her and any woman or man who has felt the same way.

First, I told Karin that she just needed to change her mind-set about it. My sister is a boss when it comes to that, but she just didn't see it as a great area of concern until we talked about it. Something about me saying that fashion should be your friend exposed an area she needed to deal with. I'm not saying that you need to turn into a shopaholic, but you must shift your mind-set from thinking of it as a chore if you will ever allow it to be the joy it can be.

How can you make exploring fashion a fun experience for you? Perhaps you might enlist the help of a friend who is fashion forward and loves to shop. We all know someone who has great fashion sense. A person who cares about you can give you ideas about things that could work for you that you might not have considered. Additionally, many department stores have personal shoppers to assist you with that too. Make it a date. Go out on a shopping excursion, and then treat them to lunch.

Take yourself in. Work that three-way mirror. Look at yourself from different angles. Take pictures of yourself when you try on different garments. This will help you see how it really looks on you. Also, having your friend with you can also give you another perspective on how it looks on you. They can see what we don't see.

Let go of any past painful experiences with fashion. It's all about your attitude and how you see the shopping excursion now. You may have had a hard time in the past finding things that delight you, but that was then. This is now. Things have changed. It's a whole new world since fashion during your childhood, or at least it can be.

I encourage you to find your favorite designers. Pay attention to the brands that have worked before. My sister and I both love Calvin Klein. I like Ralph Lauren, INC, and Fashion to Figure also. They offer clothing in a variety of bright colors. They have great style. They design fashion that is sexy and classy. The cut of their clothing works amazingly on my shape. Find your designers. Look for those brands first. It'll make it an easier process for you.

As we talked about this, Karin began to feel much more open and readier to make fashion her friend. I hope you will too.

Your Wardrobe Essentials

Time to boost your style. I'd like to give you just a few essentials that I think are must-haves for everyone's wardrobe. Although this is not an exhaustive list, it is certainly enough to build upon.

Where It All Begins

Let's go. In making your presentation runway ready, it all starts with the foundation. If the foundation of your home has cracks in it, your house could fall. We want to prevent any collapses in your presentation by making sure the foundation of your apparel is sure. Gentlemen, make sure you have underwear that is the right size and fits you. No boxers that are hanging off you or briefs that are too tight. Ouch! Ladies, the same goes for you. Your underwear should fit and be comfortable on you. If you've gained weight, get larger panties. Not only is it very uncomfortable to wear undies that are too small, but it can lead to health concerns such as yeast infections and ingrown hairs. I'm not a doctor, and this is not medical advice, but I know that you want to steer clear of that.

Here's the elephant in the room. Your clothes will look so much better on you when you wear the right bra size. Oh my goodness. Ladies, you should be getting measured at least twice a year for an accurate fit with your bra to see if your bra size or cup size has changed.

95

Your bra sets the tone for everything. It controls. It presents. It lifts and separates.

You will also need a variety of bras to wear. They could include a T-shirt bra, a plunge bra for when you may want to show a little cleavage, and an exceptional strapless bra. Your bra straps do not need to be showing outside any of your clothing. That's what strapless bras are for. Again, please invest in yourself. Stock bras in nude and black as a minimum. There are many great colors and patterns and frills and thrills in lingerie, but it's always advantageous to have seamless bras and panties in nude and black also. They often look the best under your clothing. Curvy Couture Intimates is a fave.

Get a great body smoother. Whether it is Spanx or control-top pantyhose, most women need a smoother. Maybe you need a waist cincher or something that takes in your hips and thighs a bit. All these things will allow your clothes to lay properly and your body to be smooth under it. This is not a matter of size either. I know smaller women who wear smoothers because they know how their skin looks under certain garments, and they want it to appear smoother. Years ago, women wore slips, camisoles, and girdles on a regular basis. Many of us have abandoned that, but I appreciate the wisdom of it. It allows us to present so much better.

Let me make this point here. Your inner foundation sets the tone for everything in your outer life too. What are you building on? You must address it from the ground up and from the inside out. While we are working on the outer you, continue to go back and repair some of the cracks in your inner foundation too. There may have been fractures caused in your childhood. That is true for most people. You may have had painful experiences at school. Again, that is common too. There may be cracks in your life about something that happened ten years ago or in your first marriage. You must go back and repair those breaches if you haven't, because I promise you, it is affecting you today. You don't even realize how much it's coloring your decisions and actions daily. It is altering your mental and emotional presentation in the world.

THE MODEL BAG—YOUR FUNDAMENTAL FASHION PIECES

Whenever I am out on a job, I always pack my model bag so I have items that prepare me to present myself well in almost every circumstance. I'd like to share some fashion pieces that will complete your look and allow you to present yourself beautifully.

Your Shoe Swag

All ladies should have at least a pair of stylish pumps in nude and in black. These shoes will be able to go with a wide variety of outfits. Additionally, strappy silver and gold shoes for dressier outfits are great to have. I also like to have a pair of sexy shoes that can add a pop of color to what I'm wearing. I suggest shoes in red. You also need a pair of comfortable ballet flats that can work in day or evening. Have some fashionable sneakers, a simple canvas shoe, or Chuck Taylors, which always work too for anyone. Fellas, make sure you have dress shoes in black and brown in various styles.

Jeans and Slacks

Everyone needs a favorite pair of jeans. These must have an exceptional fit. Jeans are a wardrobe staple because they are often one of our most comfortable garments and are also very versatile. You can spruce them up with a blouse and a pair of heels or dress them down with a T-shirt and sneakers. Additionally, jeans come in a variety of fits and washes to suit your individual needs.

I think gentlemen also need great pairs of black slacks and jeans. They are versatile and can be worn to work or for play and provide endless wardrobe solutions.

The T-shirts Have It

A baby T-shirt or a V-neck T-shirt. T-shirts are a wardrobe essential because, just like jeans, they are super comfortable. They are timeless, and they come in a variety of colors and fits too. A clean, crisp, white T-shirt always works and goes with almost everything. As for the necklines, if you have a short neck, go for the V-neck. If you have a long neck, stick with a crew neck.

Otherwise, take your pick. Be sure to use great fabrics like cotton. Avoid super thin fabrics.

I always feel like you can put on your favorite jeans with a simple, white V-neck T-shirt and hoop earrings for a look that is classic, chic, and cute. You might wear flats, or you could put on those red pumps with a jacket, and you're ready for a casual night out. It could even be paired with a fancy skirt or under a slip dress. The classic white T-shirt is a must-have.

The White Button-Down Shirt

No wardrobe is complete without a classic white button-down shirt. It can be worn tucked in with slacks in a business setting or untucked with rolled sleeves for hanging out on the weekend. It can be layered under sweaters and over T-shirts. Be sure to replace it each year or two. You want your white shirt to be super white.

The Little Black Dress

Every lady needs a perfect little black dress. It's amazing alone and can be made into a variety of different looks through your accessories. Have a few in varying lengths and styles for each season.

Maxis and Wraps

I also recommend that you own a few maxi dresses and as well as some wrap dresses that go to the knee, are midi length and full length. In my opinion, they flatter almost every body type. They can be worn for almost any occasion and in every season.

When Diane von Furstenberg first modeled the wrap dress back in the '70s, their marketing slogan was "Feel like a woman, wear a dress." Yesss, honey! Women felt empowered and confident as they accentuated their feminine frames in this new dress style. This timeless classic still rules today.

The Turtles

In fall and winter, I always have wonderful turtleneck dresses and turtleneck sweaters. Turtlenecks beautifully frame your face. They are like an open canvas and can provide endless styling options. They can be worn with statement jewelry or accented with beautiful scarves. I enjoy layering them, and they come in a variety of colors and textures. I love them!

Blazers and Jackets and Buttons! Oh My!

Chic and elegant blazers work for both men and women. They can pull your outfit together. You can wear them to work or for a fun night out. Men can pair a blazer with slacks or jeans. Women can match it up with jeans or a skirt or even over a cocktail dress. It's also great for that between-seasons time, when it's not quite cold enough for a heavy jacket. Sport a blazer. Make sure that it fits you and hits you where it needs to. Take your height and your build into consideration. Try different cuts of jackets. Blazers can be fitted, single- or double-breasted, have a bolero cut or be oversized, and have a variety of number of buttons or ornamentation. There are dozens of styles to choose from. Find your favorite.

A stylish jean jacket is a staple. They too come in a variety of washes, styles, and cuts. They are also extremely versatile and can be worn over a maxi dress or paired with a skirt or even leggings. I also love wearing a moto or motorcycle jacket. Try it in a different color like electric blue. I think it can give your ensemble a little bit of a cool, sexy edge.

Dazzling Dusters

Ladies, consider having a few dusters on hand. Whether it is a delicate kimono duster, which works with most body types, or a full-length duster with a bold pattern or print, they can be used to switch up an outfit, to dress it up or dress it down. They are usually knit or made from lightweight material and can be a stylish, transitional item from cooler into warmer temperatures.

My Thoughts on Other Adornment

In my model bag, I always bring various adornments. I pack diamond studs and hoops in gold and in silver. They can dress up or dress down an outfit. I also pack my own foundation and lashes. This goes back to playing with fashion and making it fun. Play with makeup. Go to makeup counters and let them make you up. Try different colors.

Experiment with color with your clothing as well. See what colors accentuate your skin tone. By all means, don't think that because you are plus size that you have to wear black. I hope those days are long gone. Wear colors that show how you feel inside—or wear colors that align with how you *wish* to feel on the inside. For instance, if you're feeling a little down, put on a bright, sunny color like yellow. It is bound to pick you up. I do believe the colors you wear affect your mood. That bright color will help to attract bright positive energy.

One of my favorite ways to play with fashion is with belts and pins or brooches. I have hijacked some of my mom's great rhinestone pins. *(Shhh.* Hope she doesn't see this.) You can overhaul a color block maxi dress and elevate it into evening wear just by adding a rhinestone pin on it. Pins and brooches can class things up and add variation to something you have worn before, which expands your wardrobe. You can make the dress look like it's something brand new by just adding accessories to it.

Hats are so much fun. You might have on a simple outfit, but adding a hat to it could take it to another level. Play with your accessories. Gloves and scarves and belts and pins make it fabulous.

Let's talk about your crowning glory—your hair, darling! Your hair is your crown, even if you decide to rock a bald head. Hair is a form of self-expression. It is another way we show the world our own beautiful personality. No matter how you choose to wear your hair, make sure that it is healthy. Whether you wear it short or long, loc'd or straight, wavy or in an afro, represent yourself at your best.

I wear a lot of wigs for work. Here's a quick tip about having fun with your hair fashion. Take a visit to a beauty supply store. Bring one of your stylish girlfriends who wears wigs herself and will tell you the truth. Try on several different wigs so you can see what cut or look flatters you the most. I would especially recommend this before doing a dramatic haircut. Why not test drive it on a wig? Wigs are a blessing if you want to change your hair color without actually changing your hair color, or before changing it.

I am a "less is more" sister when it comes to hair, but I definitely feel like hair is something you can play around and have lots of fun with and wear different styles that express yourself the most. Remember this. If you do decide to wear wigs, please do not neglect your hair underneath them. Many ladies use wigs for a protective style. It is only a protective style when you are truly maintaining the health of your natural hair underneath the wig. Keep that in mind.

Look the Part

In closing, look the part. I can't stress this enough. People pay attention when you give attention to your appearance. They want to elevate you when you show that you care. We can say what we want, but people are attracted to what looks like wealth and success. We are drawn to people who look like winners. If you want to be on a winning team, look like a winner. Look like your next level, and yes, it can be accomplished on a budget. Present your next-season look in your current season. I promise you, it will help to propel you into the next season. Look like where you are going.

If you want to be the department manager, you cannot dress like you're an intern. I think this is why style shows like *What Not to Wear* are so successful. They show people how they can be so further along in their own self-esteem and confidence if they would just dress for their body type, wear colors that work for them, dress appropriately for their station in life, and get a hair color and style that compliments them. Your presentation is your calling card; always look the part.

Runway Story Time—Look Like a Supermodel

Here's a quick story about when I wanted to make sure that my presentation was on point. I was going to the runway casting for season 14 of *Project Runway*. It would be the first time they would ever use plus models in the runway show finale, which was pretty historic. I remembered that it was a blazing, hot day in New York City. I wanted to be a cut above the rest.

I had my favorite makeup artist, Christopher Michael, come over to beat my face. My hair was freshly done too. In planning my route to the casting, I could have taken the train. The train actually would let me out right across the street from the casting, but it was too hot. I did not want to go into the casting sweating. It was one of those sunny days where my makeup would have been melting down my face. I wanted to walk in the door looking like the supermodel that I am, so I paid the extra money and took a cab. I also knew they would be taking pictures of all the models, so when they looked at my pictures, with my hair and makeup done to the nines, alongside the others, I wanted my presentation to already reflect the polished, finished work. I was willing to go the extra mile, to be above and beyond to make sure that my presentation was superb regardless of the outside factors. And I did this on the possibility of getting the job. You must do that too. Invest in your presentation. I'm sure there were other girls who were just as pretty as I was, but I know the extra effort made a difference. I'm so thankful I did, because I booked the job, and the rest is history—the first black plus model to walk in a *Project Runway* Designer Finale Showcase. Hey!

Runway Action Plan—Your Wardrobe Makeover

Whew! I'm excited! How about you? Are you ready to hit your wardrobe and do a little housecleaning? First things first. In the book entitled *The Life-Changing Magic of Tidying Up*, the author, Marie Kondo, shares how to sort through your wardrobe. She recommends you take all your clothes, shoes, coats, and accessories from every area of the house and bring them to one area, perhaps your bedroom, and lay them out in stacks according to their category.

Here are a few qualifiers before you even try Kondo's method. First, the item must fit you well. Next, it should represent where you're going. Those are the first two qualifiers as to whether they need to stay in your wardrobe. The next would be from Ms. Kondo's book. Pick up each item one by one. If it gives you joy right now, keep it. If it doesn't, sell it, discard it, or throw it away. She contends that there is no need in keeping anything that doesn't currently bring you joy. It has lived beyond its useful life for you, and you can bid it farewell.

When my sister followed this method, she went through her wardrobe and got rid of twelve large trash bags of clothes. I struggle sometimes with getting rid of things, so this helped me as well! Try it. It works.

Next, it's time to go through what is left of your wardrobe to see if you have the suggested essentials. In doing so, you can write in your journal or someplace else. Make a shopping list. Use this as your guide, and start to shop for the items you need the most. Be sure to bring that friend to go with you who can encourage you in this. And, by all means, have fun with fashion!

"As we let our light shine, we unconsciously give other people permission to do the same. As we are liberated from our own fear, our presence actually liberates others."
– Marianne Williamson

"Take responsibility for the energy you bring."
– Jill Bolte Taylor

— 4 —

MASTER PRESENCE AND POSITIVITY

PRESENCE IS THE ENERGY YOU BRING wherever you go. Every time you step into a room, you have the ability to change or set the tone for how others will react to you and how you will react to them by the presence you show up with. If you want to bring joy, be that joy. If you want to bring power, stand in your power. I know that I am St. George and Delois' child. I also know that I am God's child. There is a certain power that I stand in because I know who I am and whose I am. I am a work in progress. I know my strengths and my weaknesses. I also know that I matter, so when I come into the room, I bring the beauty of all of my presence, spiritually, emotionally, mentally, and physically, in making the world my runway.

Your "It" Factor

People tell me that even when I'm not trying to, I exude a powerful presence. I remember Ty Hunter, Beyoncé's former stylist, telling me that I didn't understand how my presence affected others. He said that when I come into a room, people are often clutching their pearls because I'm so comfortable in my body and in my identity that it makes them pay attention or even feel a little uncomfortable. That happens when you are confident.

You are just being you, but others feel insecure because they really do not feel secure about themselves. When others are unsure of themselves, my stature can make them feel even more insecure. It's not my intention. It's how they are interpreting it. I have to remind myself that it's not my job to make anyone else feel okay with my existence or theirs. I just have to be my best me, and they have to work on themselves. Here's a nugget. Stop hiding your brilliance because others are uncomfortable with it. Don't shield your shine because of other people's insecurities.

Some call this powerful presence the "It Factor." Some people are born with it, but it can certainly be cultivated in anyone. This is not about physical stature. I know women who are five feet tall who step into rooms and shake it up, just as much as I do, with the prominence of their personality and presence. It really has to do with how you want to step onto the runway of life. It's all about how you feel about yourself too. How are you going to show up?

You Choose How You Show Up

You get to choose how you show up in life. I choose to show up with a classy, cool, down-to-earth, approachable vibe. But then, there are times where I don't really want to be approached. I know how to give off that aura as well. Recently, I attended one of my niece's eighth-grade promotion ceremonies at her school. This moment was all about her, so I was not trying to attract any attention at all. I slipped off to the side to a table by myself, and people still approached me. I let them know that I was here just to love, honor, and support my niece. I was really low-key, and yet my presence still drew people to me.

Your presence is something you have to manage. How you show up as the keynote speaker of an event may be different than how you enter a space when you are coming in the role of supporting someone else's event. My presence and energy are still there. You will see my confidence. It's just in a different role.

How to Build Your Presence

How do you build your presence? It starts with you being proud of who you are, how you look, and how you feel. It comes from being present in the moment. Showing up. Being here. Fully experiencing the now. You cannot bring all of yourself here, thinking about someplace else. For us to experience the beauty of your presence, you must focus on the time and space and place that you are in right now. It gives you the chance to take advantage of the opportunity to connect with others. It allows you to be blessed and to be a blessing. It releases you to own who you are and to allow the best of you to be seen and felt. Again, the beauty is that you get to decide how you want your presence to be felt. You project that in how you carry yourself, in the way you speak, in your manner of dress, and in how you communicate your confidence and commitment to yourself with the world.

Runway Story Time

Let your presence be felt. I remember years ago walking for Lane Bryant during Full Figured Fashion Week. I was wearing a sexy two-piece leatherette lingerie set (think Madonna, LOL), with plenty of cheeks to spare, and a floor-length, flowing, sheer chiffon skirt. It was somewhat risqué for them to show, and your girl was here for it. Okay!

Honey, I walked out there in full confidence! I wanted them to feel me. I wanted them to experience how sexy I felt in the garment. I wanted them to embrace how beautiful plus-size women can be in our lingerie. I remember the crowd going wild and giving me a standing ovation. It took my breath away!

When I walked back down the runway for the finale with the CEO of Lane Bryant, I was on a high. The energy was palpable. Because of all that love I received back from the audience while making my presence felt, I did a fist pump. Honestly, it felt like the whole world was giving me a fist pump back. I knew that something momentous had occurred that evening. When you share your love and allow your presence to be felt, it comes back to you multiplied. Your presence is a seed that brings back so much more to you.

HOW WILL YOU USE YOUR PRESENCE?

We use the power of presence everywhere we go. I use it when I go out on model castings. It's the same as when you go on an interview for a job. How do you stand out from the bunch? How do you make your mark? You allow them to experience your presence in the interview, and then again, in how you follow up adds to their perception of your presence. How do you want others to experience you? It's important to step outside of yourself and see yourself. This takes a willingness to be real with yourself. You might even have to record yourself so you can hear yourself. Happy, confident people are very self-aware. Self-awareness is momentous to your realignment in life. You must be willing to pause and see yourself as you really are. Next, you must be willing to change where you need to or want to. Honestly, if it ain't working, it ain't working. Be willing to shift.

WHAT'S THE PURPOSE?

Be responsible for the energy you bring into every situation. What's the purpose of this encounter? Pay attention to what is necessary. Maximize your moment. If you're at a networking event, you can't come in as the shrinking violet. This is the time to let your presence fill the room. You want to be magnetic to the people you are there to connect with. Make sure that your presence is open and receptive. You control that. The purpose of the moment dictates the presence I stand in and how I show up. What is your goal? When you know where you want to go, you know how you need to present yourself.

PRACTICE POISE

Poise can be defined as a dignified, self-confident manner. It is the ability to be at ease in all circumstances. Maintaining your composure even in the most difficult times demonstrates the strength and grace within you. So how do you carry yourself? Does your presence exude peace or chaos? Can you hold it together under pressure? How do you recover?

Whether I have broken a shoe or tripped on the runway—trust me, it happens—I constantly remind myself to remain calm, not just on the runway but in life. That can be very difficult at times. You might have to cry and fall apart to release the energy built up inside you. That's okay. You might fall down. Just don't stay down. We all miss the mark. When I do, I try my best to remember that things almost always work out better than I even could imagine. That centers me and allows me to relax and trust the process. There is a process we all have to go through. It's not always fun or easy, but if I can make a decision to carry myself with a sense of poise, my presence will always be felt in a positive way. Also, I always come out as a winner. That's just who I am. It's who you are too.

"Modeling is acting without words through the beauty of fashion."
– Liris

Runway Story Time—Balance Yourself

I'd love to share a little with you about how poise also encompasses balance. Balance is vital on the runway. You don't want to under-perform, and you certainly don't want to overdo it either. You must execute with balance in how you choose to display an item or how you decide to carry yourself in the process. I balanced the choices I made so my presence could be felt and experienced in a positive light all throughout my time on *Project Runway* during season 16. I had so much fun during that season.

Whether it was the shadow from the fist pump behind the screen before I emerged onto the runway when I wore designer Kenya Freeman's outfit for the Warrior Fashion Challenge or the series of spins that I worked the end of the runway with, I made sure I gave a full serving of my presence with poise to allow myself to stand out without doing the way most. Be strategic with your presence.

I did the same with the Shopkins World Challenge when I modeled designer Ayana Ife's outfit. First of all, let's be clear it was in my favorite color—pink! Also, I love feeding my inner princess with love, so the cartoon character that I created on the runway was right up my alley. This was pure joy. From the playful facial expression to the slight leaning pose, I used my sense of poise and balance to make the character and the garment come to life. It would have been easy to overdo it and make the outfit look corny or silly, but I made sure that it was evened and still firmly said fashion. My poise was a great balancing act of actress meets model. I've always said that modeling is acting without words through the beauty of fashion.

My poise was on display during the Descending Into Good and Evil Challenge when I worked with designer

Michael Brambila. I wanted to give them a "Queen of the Damned" vibe. I accomplished that through my majestic yet mysterious expressions and the dramatic effect of my turns on the runway. In life, work it with all your might. All drama is not negative. Know when to bring a little more sizzle into your presence so you can leave a lasting impression. Use your poise to your advantage.

PACE

Pace is so important, again, not just on the runway but in life. I believe that your pace is determined by finding your rhythm. My rhythm is not the same as your rhythm. My pace is not the same as yours, but when I find the tempo of my life, everything comes together. It's interesting, the longer you live, the more you appreciate when life was so much simpler. I remember being a young girl wanting to be a teenager. I can also recall being a teenager wishing that I was in my '20s. You get it?

Why are we here always wanting to be there? I have since learned to watch the pace of my life because it has a direct impact on my presence. I know there will be times when life goes at a frenetic pace. That's seasonal. It's impossible to maintain a sense of balance in life when you're always on full tilt.

This is something I always tell the participants in my Life of a Working Model Boot Camp. Pace yourself. On the runway or on the runway of your life, pace yourself. Take a moment. Find your flow. As the saying goes, "Rome wasn't built in a day." Neither will your greatness be either. Stop and smell the roses. Take a moment to make eye contact and smile at a stranger. Read to a child in your life. Call an elderly loved one just to check in. Slow down. Experience the beautiful presence of others in your life.

For more on my workshops, go to www.lirisc.com/loawmbc.

"Your attitude determines your altitude."
– Zig Ziglar

PRESENCE AND YOUR 'TUDE

So much of our presence is projected in our attitude. Your attitude is everything! Have you ever met someone, and although you haven't spent a whole lot of time with them, you just have a really good feeling about them? They are positive and cheerful, and you feel good in their presence. More than likely, they have projected a positive attitude.

Your presence can be felt when you walk in the room. Others can sense things about you without you saying a word. It carries that much weight. We all must be willing to check ourselves from time to time and to look at the man or woman in the mirror. Am I reflecting the best of who I am? I'm not a fan of comparison, especially with others, however, when I compare myself with the best version of myself, where am I measuring up? Do I need to make adjustments? Be willing to do them.

It's true. Your attitude does indeed determine your altitude. How high or how low you go is determined by the manner in which you carry yourself. A great attitude can open doors for you. Talent is never enough. Even in the very visual profession in which I am, sometimes the most beautiful girls have the worst attitudes, and they no longer look so beautiful to us. We've all seen reality shows where some of the women looked spectacular on the outside, but their attitude toward others made us cringe. Don't let that be you, Boo. Give yourself a checkup from the neck up. Get real and honest with yourself. How's your attitude about life? About yourself? About your own abilities? About your friends and loved ones? About your career and business opportunities? Elevate your attitude, and elevate your life. It will make you stand out from the crowd and be the light that you were created to be. Be the light. Be the change you wish to see. Let's talk about positivity in your presence.

"Be the change you want to see in the world."
– Ghandi

Positive, Confident, and Successful

Be positive. In my world, it's very easy to fall into negativity. There's so much rejection encountered in a working model's life. You get some castings, but there many more you don't. Sometimes you do well on the runway. Other times, you don't. There are times when you get beautiful pieces to model, and other times you won't. For every plus, there are negatives. It's easy to become very pessimistic, so it is imperative for me to immerse myself in positivity so I can live in joy and peace and keep my spirit clean and clear. I must watch my presence at all times.

We all face difficult situations on the runway of life. Positivity helps us to keep our minds when we feel like losing them. I stay positive by reminding myself of all the great things I did to prepare for the fruits I am reaping or will reap. It keeps me on track with my passion too. We forget how much power we have. We are so mighty. We can build ourselves up, or we can tear ourselves down.

Watch Your Words

My mom always says that "words are spirit and words are so powerful, so speak life." The Bible says that "death and life is in the power of the tongue." I have the power to speak death over people and situations just as much as I have the power to speak life over them. Watch the words that you speak to and about others and yourself.

Watch Your Thoughts

Even before I speak it, what am I thinking? How are you thinking about others? Believe it or not, this affects your presence with them. What we speak out of our mouth comes from what we are thinking. If I am training my mind to be positive despite what's going on, it causes me to always see the silver lining in life, with others and myself. I'm always seeing that it's another day and another fresh start. Positivity conditions me to find alternatives when I come up against obstacles or roadblocks in life. It helps me to shoot down those negative thoughts and replace them with positive ones.

Supercharge It!

Positivity gives you an added boost in your performance no matter what's happening. It's supercharges your presence and life. It's almost like being in a video game where you never run out of lives. Positivity strengthens your faith. It's a shield. It's like vibranium. It causes negativity to bounce off you so that your presence is strong and vibrant. Positivity is vital to confidence because it empowers you with resilience. You can take a licking and keep on ticking. Disaster may strike, but you know it's not over. You can get knocked down but still get right back up again.

KEEP HOPE ALIVE

When you are positive, your presence emanates hope. You might not get the job you thought you would, but if you are positive in your mind-set, you believe the right position is finding you. It's just a matter of time. You have patience because you know it's coming. You believe that when it's all said and done, it's all for your good. People are drawn to that hopeful, positive presence.

I GOT THIS!

In modeling, since we hear *no* far more than we hear *yes*, we must be extremely positive to be successful, working models. I think this is true of any endeavor in life. In modeling, it's not possible to encounter so many closed doors and keep at it without your powerpack of positivity and presence. Your positivity has to be on fleek. Positivity is your "I Got This," in spite of, attitude: *This job didn't come through, but another will. They didn't book me today, but my booking is coming. This relationship didn't work out, but I learned some things that have made me ready for "The One." I got this!*

SIDE NOTE. *I don't believe there is only open person who can be ideal for you. Just using the expression, LOL. Remember that. There are many Ones.*

Runway Story Time—Hello?

I want to share a little story about my dad and positivity. Maybe you don't know this, but I am what we call in the church community a "PK." For those of you who may not know what that means, I am a preacher's kid, or a pastor's kid. Yes, that's me. My dad was a pastor for over forty years. He's retired now. I have seen and experienced so many things inside and outside the church because of my dad's position, and I have learned so many lessons about people and how we tick.

Dad really has a heart of gold. He has always wanted to reach people with the love of God and to be a positive force in the life of anyone he encounters. I remember years ago when he got this great idea to use a tele-calling machine to spread positive messages of hope throughout our community via telephone. It would randomly call numbers and play a word of encouragement to people.

I cannot tell you how many people would call the number back to thank him. People would stop him in the community to share their stories with us. They may have been deep in depression, feeling hopeless or even suicidal when their phone rang. They answered the phone, and instead of getting a person, his taped message spoke life into them. It may have been the only positive thing they had encountered in a while, and it changed their lives. I didn't know it then, but my father was creating a presence of hope and positivity in me through his ministry, his outreaches, and his own positive attitude of faith. He never gives up, even when others think he's crazy. That's happened a lot. He just keeps on going. I am forever grateful to him because of that example he's lived before me.

"The most important decision we make is whether we believe we live in a friendly or hostile universe."
– Albert Einstein

"Perception is reality."
– Unknown

MANAGE YOUR PERCEPTIONS

To keep your presence pure, you must positively manage your perceptions. What is perception? It is the way you use your senses or mind to interpret or understand something. We think of reality as being real, actual, or factual. Unfortunately, what we see as reality is not always so. Our perception, how we personally see things, is our reality for us, whether it is true or not. This is why we must be intentional about positively managing our perceptions.

What you see is not always true or real. Two people can look at the same situation and see two totally different things because they are two different people with varying viewpoints and experiences. To live in the realm of possibility, it is imperative for you to remove any negative filters and mind-sets and to minimize or eliminate any unfavorable memories or experiences that could color your worldview against you.

It reminds me of the wonderful filters we have on our phones. Sometimes we take pictures and they come out a little flat. That's where the filters come into play. They can turn an average picture into a fabulous one. The brightness increases. The colors pop. You can even smooth out imperfections on your face and whiten your teeth with filters. Make positivity your filter. Learn to look at things through a positive eye. Intentionally search for the good.

Do you see the glass of your life as half full or half empty?

You must develop a half-full mentality. Many days when I go out for a job, I face "rejection." I put rejection in quotes because I have the responsibility of monitoring how I see it. Not getting a job may mean that I just didn't have the look they needed for the shot. It's not anything against me at all. That's how I see it. It doesn't diminish who I am or what I have to offer. It doesn't mean I did anything wrong either. *No* does not always mean *never.* Remember that. Be careful to see the experiences of your life in a positive light. By seeing the glass as half full, my expectation is always on fullness and not emptiness. We get to decide which universe we live in. Is it a friendly universe or a hostile universe? How we perceive it is how it will be. Be positive.

MONITOR YOUR SELF-TALK

In addition to managing your perceptions or how you see things, you must watch what you say. I have a question for you. Who do you talk to the most? Think about your life. Who has your ear more than anyone else? The answer is pretty obvious. You do!

There is no one's voice you hear more than your own. What are you saying to yourself about yourself? How are you talking about the past? What are you saying about your present? What are your words projecting into your future? What tapes are you creating in your life to play over and over? Your world is being framed by your words. Do you like the picture you see? Speak Life. It's up to you to monitor what you are saying to yourself and whether it is what you want or what you don't want.

Runway Story Time—Change Those Tapes

Recently, I had the pleasure of taking my big sister on a trip to Jamaica to celebrate her birthday. Her birthday was several months earlier, but we were both too busy to mesh our calendars to do our girls' trip together. When an opening came, I booked it, and within a couple of weeks we were on our way to beautiful, sunny Ocho Rios.

One balmy afternoon, we were seated at the swim-up bar when a woman and a gentleman across the pool bar waved at us. We waved back, and they came over to join us for a little chitchat. They were so warm and friendly. It was a pleasure meeting them. Within moments we found out they were there to celebrate her daughter's graduation from high school. She was a proud mama and beamed with joy about how lovely and accomplished her daughter was. There was only one thing that troubled her about her beautiful baby girl. Because her daughter was plus size, although she was very likable, popular, smart, super active at her school in school government, and had received awards for school spirit, they believed no one was interested in dating her because of her weight.

Right away, I told her mom that that could not be true. There are plenty of plus-size women in loving relationships all over the world. Soon, her delightful daughter swam over to join us. As we connected over fashion, I shared with her some great sites to find swimwear, evening wear, and day-to-day fashions. Finally, we had broken enough ice for me to really say what I wanted to convey.

"You must change the tapes you're playing in your mind about yourself," I told her. "You are beautiful. There is someone who will love you for all the beauty that you are. If you continue to say that no one wants me because I am plus size, although that is not true, that's what you'll have." Not only did she have to change the tape playing in her head, she also had to eliminate the words that were keeping her from what she wanted. She did not even realize she was giving off a signal of being unwanted, which was in the way of anyone expressing desire for her. Our beliefs are out of us whether we realize it or not. I gave her my email address so I could actually send her the links to the plus designers and fashion sites we talked about.

The next day I received an email from her thanking me profusely. She told me she really appreciated meeting me and talking with me. What brought tears to my eyes was that she had thought about all I said to her, and she wrote, "Please know that you changed a young girl's life." In all that I do, I want to be a light and an inspiration to others to live life fully and confidently. I think she's on the road to that. If I had only come to Jamaica to change her life, it was worth it.

Watch your thoughts. Monitor your self-talk. Your mind and your mouth are powerful, and they affect your presence for good or for bad. Sometimes we have belief systems that are like old, dusty tapes playing in our minds. We don't even realize how much we have bought into something simply because we continue to rehearse those lines in our head. If you want to know what you think or what you believe, look at your life. Speak to yourself with love and kindness. Talk about what you want and not what you don't want, and allow the universe to manifest it in your life.

Performances That Pop

It is so important that you positively evaluate your performance. Whenever we improve our skills and are able to perform at a higher level, it raises our confidence and, thus, how we show up. We cannot get better if we won't pay attention to where we are right now and make a positive assessment of it.

Earlier I mentioned about a runway show that I did in Barcelona. I make it a habit to go back and watch the footage of my runway shows. I look for things I did well and things I can improve upon. How can you be your best without positively assessing your performance?

Many times, we look in the mirror of life just like we do in a regular mirror. Too often we're looking to see what's wrong, to straighten things up. I would love to encourage you to look at your life and your performances in life with eyes of kindness and compassion.

When I looked at my runway footage from Barcelona, I realized something. I was walking too quickly, but I also saw my greatness too. My posture was stately and erect. My expressions were soft and beautiful. I loved my hand placement. My spins were on point. The looks over my shoulder were captivating. Overall, it was popping even though I needed to slow down a bit. Try it. There is always so much good in every situation in life if you'll just look for it.

Take inventory of your life. Whether it is on the runway, with your relationships, or in your career, healthy self-review allows you to improve. Sometimes we feel like we are building, but we are doing so on an unstable foundation. You must reinforce and fortify your foundation by looking at what you've done before. Maybe this will help you. Evaluation is not negative or positive. It just is. The meaning is what we give to it. Be honest in your assessment, but look for twice as much good as you do otherwise. It will help you to stay positive. Take account of it and then let it go. Keep it moving.

> *"You can't let fear paralyze you. The worst that can happen is you fail, but guess what: You get up and try again. Feel that pain, get over it, get up, dust yourself off and keep it moving."*
> *– Queen Latifah*

DROP PERFECTIONISM

I have a bit of a perfectionist streak in me at times. I found myself getting really downcast or even sometimes depressed about things not going as I expected. I was letting myself drown in it. After I did a bit of self-evaluation, I realized I was being too hard on myself. I saw I was being really unfair to myself. I didn't deserve that. I wanted things to be just so, right, perfect. It was really holding me back from what could be happening next in my life. I had to learn that perfection does not exist. Perfect *for me*, however, does exist. Perfect for me is me doing my very best at all times, and that is enough. Can you accept that your best is enough?

QUICKLY RECOVER

Learning to quickly recover was a big lesson for me in positivity. When I stumble, like we all do, I make a decision to quickly get over it. Maybe I will give myself twenty-four hours or a few days. Honestly, sometimes a little bit of sulking helps me to release it. This may not sound very positive, but it is for me. I believe that when we suppress emotions and act like they are not there, we're setting ourselves up for failure. We are bound to repeat it because we haven't allowed ourselves to feel it and gain the lessons. Allow yourself to let go of the emotional baggage, whether it is in your relationships or in your work life. It's okay to feel the way you feel, even in your darkest moments. Unpack your bags and decide to release it.

Another thing to be careful of is compartmentalizing things. While there are some bags that may take a while to unpack, make sure you don't have emotional baggage from years and years ago just sitting around your emotional house, accumulating. That's when we can slip into denial or repression. Let's not push it to the side or stack it up in the back of our minds and hearts and act like it's not there. I don't know about you, but I don't want to be blocked, stuck, or sad. I allow myself to feel whatever I need to feel. If I have to lay in the floor and cry or stay in the bed for two days, I do it so that I can move on. Be aware of your own grieving process. Tune In. Ask yourself, "Am I holding on to this longer than I need to? Is this stalling my progress in life?" If so, it's time to deal with it so you can move forward. Be patient with yourself. And, by all means, get help. Sometimes in certain communities we ignore the fact that our mental health may need to be supported by a professional. A skilled therapist is your friend. If you need one, go and get one. Forgive. Let go. Quickly recover. Remain positive in your process, and be free.

> *"If you try to follow everyone else's mold, you'll probably fail at some point because God created us uniquely for a reason."*
> *- Queen Latifah*

Do You

I'd like to share a few more practical tips about building your presence. There's nothing that wreaks havoc on your presence than pretending. I'm not referring to when you're making a faith move. I mean straight being a fraud. More than anything, be you and do you. You can only be confident at being the real you. That is not to say you will not have to build belief in the process of revealing or becoming the real you, but imitating what you are not never works. You are very special and were meant to be in the world at this time for a purpose. Your presence in the Earth is necessary, and we need your presence to show through. You are the answer to someone's question. You are the solution to someone's problem. Your presence makes someone else's life better. Show up as you—the bold, beautiful, confident you.

BE PRESENT

A powerful part of your presence is found in your being present. Be in the here and now. Stand in your present power. We can spend so much time living in the past that we miss all the wonderful moments happening right now. Good, bad, or indifferent, there's no value in constantly living in the past. It can rob you of your joy. Conversely, we can spend so much time worrying about the future or even fantasizing about the future without present action. That can cause us to fail to appreciate our current good or to make significant strides toward manifesting what we desire. This is the epitome of being stuck. Neither extreme is beneficial. I believe that being truly grateful and living your best life right now actually creates your fabulous future.

Being present is about being in tune with your truth and living from it. It involves pouring your whole self into your life. It is about recognizing your assignment in the Earth. It includes centering yourself, especially when you sense you have gotten off course. Presence is about knowing when to stop and take a break when you feel stressed. It is being still and resting or breathing if your body or mind calls for it. It's not about denying where you are but about embracing it and loving yourself, the situation, and those in your life too.

ENGAGE. CONNECT.

Live in presence with those in your life. Authentically engage. In day-to-day life and even in my travels, I will often meet people who have been following my career for years. I stop and really try to give them a moment of presence to feel me and to feel my energy. I will usually ask their name and have a quick conversation with them. I may reach out and give them a hug because I want them to know and to feel that I am just like they are. I just have a job that puts me in the public's eye. I think it is so important to connect with others. It is a path to growth and change.

This actually reminds me of the runway. There is no joy in being on it alone with no one to watch you or to walk with you. On the runway, I am offering an outfit, but I am selling a lifestyle. I am selling a moment. I am selling you a fantasy or a dream. I am also pouring out a piece of myself and hoping that you will receive it, appreciate it, and experience my presence. The same must be true for you. Don't be afraid to be present, to take in the moments, to experience life in all of its guts and glory and use them to expand yourself. Connect. Engage. Live! Being present is living in the spirit of love day in and day out. Be present.

FIND YOUR VOICE

To walk in your true presence, you must find your voice. It's imperative that you know what you believe. What do you stand for? What do you value? We all must come to that crossroad in life when we make choices for ourselves. This is the time when we have to challenge all of the beliefs handed down by our parents, our culture, and society and find what's true for ourselves.

Another part of your presence is finding your own sound. Listen to the beat of your own drum. To be successful, your authenticity must be a priority to you. You will never be able to speak a truth that isn't yours. You will never be able to move confidently living a life that belongs to someone else. We spent a lot of time looking at goals and dreams and visions earlier in the book. I invite you to go back to your journal. Read what you have written. Is this truly your vision, or is it someone else's? If it really is yours, are you afraid to make it known or to let your voice be heard? Why? You must be willing to take the risk of not being understood or accepted to find your voice and speak your truth. It is only then that your true tribe can emerge to support you.

YOUR BODY SPEAKS

Perhaps you've heard this before, but your communication is comprised of much more than your words alone. It's not just what you say, it's how you say it. When it comes to living in the presence of confidence, your body language accounts for a great deal of that. Your body is always speaking a language without words. It is affecting how you think and feel. I use my body for a living. How I stand or sit or walk or move makes a world of difference based on what I am trying to convey. That's true for you too. Let me explain.

Your posture—not only does it affect how you look, your posture affects how you feel. It determines whether you exude confidence. Stand tall no matter how tall you are. I don't care if you are four feet tall or six feet tall. As an example, when people get together to take pictures, tall people will start to bend down to blend in with their shorter counterparts, and shorter people are standing on tiptoes to appear taller. Unfortunately, we are often unconscious as to how it makes us look when we do that. So, here's the question. Are you doing the same thing in life? Are you crouching to fit into the crowd? Is your inner posture huddled instead of tall? Stand in the power of who you are in all things.

Be Grateful for the Skin You're In

Be grateful for your beautiful body. You are in the body God gave you, and it is magnificent. Always be thankful for the body that you are in, regardless of its size, shape or stature. If you were meant to be tall, you would have been tall. If you were supposed to be short, you would have been short. Be grateful for the skin that you are in.

You never know who's watching you, whether it is your future life partner or a future business partner. Hold your head high. It is an honor to be you. Square your shoulders. The world is your oyster. If you don't carry yourself like a king or queen in these streets or stand like one, no one will experience your presence as it either. Even if you don't feel it yet, just changing your physiology alone can cause you to feel that way instantly and over time.

Step in with Confidence

I always try to step into a place or an event with confidence, whether I am wearing jeans, sweats, or a fabulous gown. It's almost like your handshake. I don't need to squeeze a person's hand so hard that it feels like I'm breaking it. That would be overdoing it. I also don't need to give you the limp dead-fish handshake either, because that would appear weak. A nice firm handshake is just right. It communicates confidence and self-assurance. It's the same thing with our posture. Think of it this way: the queen of England doesn't come into a room wondering what you think about her—it doesn't matter. She steps in with the confidence of "I am the queen."

POSTURE AND POSE

How you use your body tells a story about you. As a part of my Life of a Working Model Boot Camp, I have a special workshop called Perfection in Posing. What's great is people from all walks of life take these day-long boot camp workshops because they know that being able to express confidence through their body is vitally important to their success.

In the workshop, I teach on two types of posing with the attendees. First, there is editorial posing, which is what you might see more in magazines. It is more structured, avant-garde, and artsy. Second, the commercial catalog posing is more friendly, natural, and fluid. It's inviting and exemplifies a lifestyle for people to buy into. These styles are different in their execution and attitudes. Your posture and your posing will vary. How you sit and how you hold your body will vary. Your personality photo poses will be different than the pose in your speaker photos. The purpose is different. It is giving off a language or a signal from how you pose your body.

Why is this important? As a model, how I pose affects the whole tenor of the photo shoot and how the pictures are perceived. It's my job to capture the intended message and convey it with my posture and my poses. It's amazing to watch in the boot camps how I can give them one little trick that changes everything. It could be about their posture or even in their hand placement for a certain pose. Something that small changes the whole energy of the shot. It can also totally transform their signal and aura, which gives the picture a whole new look. Remember, on the runway of life, people are always reading you. What is your body language saying? You may not be posing, but how are you holding yourself? How you pose affects not only your perception but also others' perspective of you too.

TAKE UP SPACE

Confident people take up space. We are not hunched in a corner trying to make ourselves smaller. When we feel powerful, we expand. We lift our arms in victory like we've just crossed a finish line. Think Usain Bolt. We stretch out. We do a fist pump, like I did at the end of the runway show. I have observed that men are often taught to be more self-assured and confident. Women, at least in western culture, are often taught to be more externally validated and to people please. I remember seeing a Dove Soap commercial that highlighted how much women said "I'm sorry." Clip after clip showed beautiful, strong women almost apologizing for their existence. *You bump into me, and I apologize. I need to say something, so I apologize first.* No, ladies! It's time for us to take a confident stand for ourselves, our voices, and our value. Don't apologize for taking up space. It's why you're here. Take it!

On the Power Train

I'm a New Yorker. This is funny, but I always notice the difference between how men and women take up space on the train. As women, we're often socialized to be nice and not to infringe on other people's space. Many of the sisters are bunched up on the train, having their legs closed tightly with ankles crossed and arms purposely on the inside of their body on their lap. On the other hand, men are often stretched out, just as relaxed, with their legs open and all over into your space. Is that rudeness, or do they just naturally expand?

I think it's a power play. I'm fascinated by the work of Amy Cuddy. You can find her online with her famous TED Talk on this subject. Her research found that powerful people are more confident, assertive, and optimistic. We actually feel like we are going to win, even when we're just playing games with others. Cuddy stated that powerful people often think more abstractly and are willing to take more risks. In her studies, they found that by just adopting powerful poses with their body for as little as two minutes, it caused the testosterone levels of their participants to rise and their cortisol levels to decrease. That's important because most dominant alpha leaders have higher testosterone and lower cortisol. They're able to stand up and confidently lead and take control, but from a place of ease.

Your physiology affects how you think and feel. Cuddy says, "Our bodies can change our minds. Our minds can change our behavior. Our behavior changes our outcomes." She shares a very touching story about how, during her college years, she was in a terrible accident and sustained a traumatic head injury, which lead to a severe drop in her IQ. This shook her sense of identity since she was always seen as gifted. She had to drop out of college, and it took her four more years to graduate. She had to work really hard, and from Princeton to Harvard, she just didn't feel like she belonged there anymore. Things changed when she realized this. So she could fake it until she could make it. I'd say, "Faith it until you make it." You can do too. By faith, use your body like a confident, self-assured, assertive person until you become it. Let your body help your transformation. I love her story. Look it up. There's a reason why it's had over 14 million views.

Ask Yourself...

Grab your journal and get to writing.

— What is my body language communicating?

— If I was confident and successful, how would I hold my body?

— How would I move if I felt powerful?

— How would I walk if I totally believed in myself?

Pick up your pace. Walk just a little faster. Put a little pep in your step. Lift your head. Smile. Loosen up. Release the stress in your body. Be open. Expand. All these things help you to look more confident and, more importantly, to feel more confident. Stand tall. Walk with confidence. Be the authority that you are.

Runway Action Plan

I want to encourage you to check out Amy Cuddy's TED Talk for yourself. Look at it at least twice. Take notes on it. Record the power poses. Then, at least twice a day or as needed, take two minutes and do your power poses. Record in your journal how you feel after doing them and how they made an impact on whatever situation you were in.

*"Success is walking from failure to failure
with no loss of enthusiasm."*
– Winston Churchill

*"Passion is energy. Feel the power that comes from
focusing on what excites you."*
– Oprah

— 5 —

FUEL YOUR PASSION AND PERSISTENCE

PASSION IS THE BURNING FLAME INSIDE YOU. It is the thing you can become slightly obsessed over. It is what you would give everything for. Passion is what you love so much that it consumes you. Growing up, I would watch hours and hours of fashion TV. I constantly read books about modeling and fashion. I poured over magazines. It totally consumed me.

Passion is the thing you would do for free. In many cases, you are doing it free before you are able to monetize it. It is the same fire that empowers you to go through the difficult times because you love it so much. It's like the trick candles on a birthday cake. Have you ever been the recipient of this joke? They bring the beautiful cake before you, and it's full of lit candles. You blow and blow and blow, but as you blow the flames, they may flicker, but they come back on again. That's passion. No matter what happens, it's still burns within you. It still drives you. It still ignites your soul. Passion never goes out.

PAY ATTENTION

Sometimes it can be difficult to figure out what we are truly passionate about. Society and even well-meaning family and friends influence us and can talk us out of what we're really passionate about. If you feel unsure about your passion, look at what you're great at. What do others say that you do amazingly well? What brings you joy? I mentioned earlier, in chapter 1, "Living in Your Purpose," to watch the glimpses. This concept bears repetition. Please pay attention to what drives you. Our passion is sometimes so obvious that we overlook it. We discount it. We stifle it for a variety of reasons, but true passion cannot be denied. It will show up again and again and again and again. Your purpose and your passion are intricately connected.

I longed to be a supermodel. The passion for it burns within me from childhood.

Runway Action Plan—Ask Yourself...

You know the routine. Grab your journal, and let's write.

— What does your heart and soul burn to do?

— What do you want to do so much that you would do it for free and often do just because you love it? (Hint—you don't have to do it for free.)

— What do you do that you can get so engrossed in you lose all track of time? When do you feel like you are in a state of flow?

— What about the world makes you feel so angry that you just have to do something about it?

— If you won $100 million in the lottery, what would you do with the rest of your life in order to feel fulfilled?

— What was your deepest pain in life?

— When do you feel like you are your best self? Your most authentic self?

— When do you feel the happiest? The freest?

— What would you love to be known for (your legacy)?

— What do you find extremely interesting or fascinating? What piques your curiosity?

— What do you love the most about yourself?

— Who do you admire? Why?

— If you died tomorrow, what would you most regret not doing?

Each of these questions should reveal something to you. They will show you some of your fire. They are divulging your desires. Pay attention to them, and act on them.

Runway Story Time

Here's a story that I share in my Life of Working Model Boot Camps. I remember when my dad was running for congress in our hometown. A photographer came to the house to take pictures of us for Dad's campaign brochures. He photographed Dad, and he took pictures of us as a family. Then he asked, "Do you mind if I take pictures of your daughter (me) by herself?" Mom replied, "Sure," so he took pictures of me. After a week or two, he came back with the photographs. (There were no digital cameras back then, only regular film that had to be developed and printed out, LOL.)

I remember him bringing the pictures and saying about me, "She's really photogenic. She should model." I remember that to this day. That gentleman watered the seed that was already in me, the passion to model. His words fanned the flame for me. I was interested in pictures, modeling, makeup, and hair, but his words ignited something within me from that moment on. He planted his seed in me that said, *You can do it. You'll be okay going after this.* In elementary school, I remember feeling this fire in me.

LIGHT YOUR FIRE

I realize that sometimes you may not see the flames of passion. This is where you must be willing to light your own fire. You must be willing to go out on a limb to get the fruit. You've got to be intentional about lighting your fire. It will involve trying new things. You must be willing to take risks. You must be curious. You have to be willing to look inside yourself and see what's there. It's great when someone else acknowledges something in you, but you must see it too. Are you willing to light your own fire?

Fire starts with a spark. The Bible says, "Do not despise the day of small beginnings." Everything great started out small. Take yourself, for instance. You started out as just a sparkle in your mother and father's eyes, which led to a fire that yielded you. Yesss! Sparks start small, but they can become great.

If you've ever had a fireplace, you know that sometimes one of the most difficult things is getting the fire started. Once it's started, you keep it going by continuing to put more logs on the fire. You have to feed the fire.

Just Start

Just start—that's what I did. I fanned the flames in me by starting small. The most important thing is that I started. Begin where you are. I didn't begin my life on international runways. Hardly! I started by doing mall fashion shows in Baltimore. And I kept the dream ablaze by working in small local modeling troupes. Be willing to start small. Be open to beginning exactly where you are.

Sometimes our greatest pain is a part of our passion and purpose. It is what God will use in us to bring hope and healing in the Earth. Let's say you were a teen mother and had to overcome many adversities to get to the life you have today. Now you have a passion for helping these young mothers. You can't just *talk* about it—you must *be* about it. Your life's tests have become your testimony so that you can help someone else. Go volunteer somewhere. Get in the game. Be a mentor to a young mother.

Where you are is right where you need to be. Decide to maximize it, and move forward with passion.

"Your obsession will become your possession."
– Ed Mylett

Pursuit

Pursuit means that you have to go after it. Passion is followed by pursuit. Passion will not allow you to stand idly on the sidelines of life. It drives you to go for it. When you have a real passion on the inside, and you believe in it, it compels you to pursue it.

I'm sure there are many people who find modeling, or whatever their job or business is, interesting. Interest is not enough. It must be an almost all-consuming obsession. Note that I said *almost*. I certainly believe in balance in your life. No one thing should totally consume your life, but I do believe there are seasons when you may become unbalanced while you're going for the dream. Your obsession will become your possession. What you become almost obsessed with having and pursuing you will achieve.

IT'S LIKE BEING IN LOVE

I'm talking about when you have such an intense desire for something that comes so naturally for you that you lose track of time in the presence of your passion. It reminds me of being in love. Your lover consumes your thoughts. You want to talk to them all the time. Being in their presence is like ecstasy. When you have a passion so deep and so true, it's like being smitten. You can't get enough. Because of that, you will go all out and put all your chips in the center of the table, placing all bets on you. When you can identify a passion that strong, pursuing it is as natural as breathing. You will do whatever it takes to make it work for you. That's the essence of pursuit.

GET IMMERSED

Immerse yourself in the culture of your passion. I always encourage those new and emerging models who attend my Life of a Working Model Boot Camps to join model Meetup groups. Join a modeling club. Take modeling workshops. Join online groups for models. In making the world your runway, you should do the same thing regarding your career. Connect with others through professional organizations. If you're passionate about a hobby, do likewise. If you love to knit, join a local knitting club. Learn new skills. Get better at it. Take it up a notch.

Create. Innovate. Be willing to reinvent yourself. Sometimes we fall into a rut because we've been doing something for a very long time and haven't grown in it. The same is true for our personal relationships. You must be intentional about keeping your relationships fresh, like making sure that your marriage is hot. Passion and pursuit are needed there for sure. Fan the flames.

> *"Nothing in this world can take the place of persistence. Talent will not; nothing is more common than unsuccessful men with talent. Genius will not; unrewarded genius is almost a proverb. Education will not; the world is full of*

educated derelicts. Persistence and determination
alone are omnipotent."
– Calvin Coolidge

"Do one thing every day that scares you."
– Eleanor Roosevelt

"The key to my longevity is that I make it work.
I make it work for me."
– Liris

PERSISTENCE

Persistence is key in going for your dreams and creating success in your life. For me, it was an absolute necessity. The average model's career lifespan is five years. I have been blessed to last far longer, largely due to persistence. I have had to stay the course. I've been strategic about how I invented and reinvented myself. Additionally, I've aimed to offer a premium product. I am committed to putting out great pictures and social media posts and to use my voice in a positive way. Those are necessary too.

IT'S YOUR TIME

Persistence is vital, because I do believe in God's timing for everything. I believe we all have our own times and seasons. We all go through different waves. There will be mountain highs and valley lows. Persistence helps you to ride the waves without allowing yourself to become discouraged. While you are working and waiting, you must condition your mind to persist and to keep your eye on the vision. Stay the course.

TRY AND TRY AGAIN

Persistence is trying again even after a negative response. I work to constantly update my look. Maybe the client is looking for a different hairstyle. Perhaps they need to see me in a different light. You have to be willing to go back to the drawing board. I need to constantly go back and say, "Take another look. Check out my new walk." We are always changing. People change their perspectives. Clients' needs will change. You never know when they're finally ready for you. Be there to get the booking. Staff can change at a company. A new set of eyes could make all difference. You never know, so it pays to be persistent and to keep trying. Send your resume again. Call the company again. Put an offer out again. You have to keep going and going and going, just like the Energizer Bunny.

DELAY IS NOT DENIAL

There was a client who I wanted to work with for quite some time, Evans out of the UK. I connected with a contact there when I walked in Full Figured Fashion Week NY, but it still took me three years of nurturing this relationship before I was able to work with them. I had to continue to believe despite the rejections. I had it on my vision board, so I kept it in front of me. I saw it day after day for years before it came to pass, which it finally did. The delay did not mean denial. It did not mean I would never work with them, just not right at that point. Because I believed, I knew it would happen. You have to put those words before you. Delay is not denial. I will not be denied. Doors will open, and I will be ready to walk through them.

Runway Story Time—Forge Your Own Path

Follow your passion and persistently forge your own path. When I started modeling, I got a lot of interest, but many of them were saying the same thing. They wanted me to be smaller and smaller, right out of high school. When I moved to New York to pursue modeling, I went to Model Search America (now Mogull Talent), since they told me if I was ever in New York to come by and see them. I'm so thankful for all that did to help me launch. I went to the office. They took my measurements and a few pictures. They explained that I wasn't the standard size, but they could recommend me to an agency that had people who looked like me.

At the time, I had never heard of plus-size modeling. I didn't even know it existed. They sent me to Wilhelmina Models—and I did know who they were. Wilhelmina Models is one of the biggest agencies in the world. I was elated. I saw the board for the plus models division. At that time, it was called 10/20, now the Curve division. The women looked like the women in my family. They were beautiful, with just a little more meat on their bones. I thought to myself, if I have to be categorized in this division, so be it. So, right out of the gate, the first agency that saw me signed me. God's favor!

While this was wonderful, I still took into consideration who I was. I knew I had to forge my own path. I was black, I was curvy, and I was young. I had to ask myself, "Where can I make my presence known?" That's when I pursued music videos and working for urban brands, along with my agency work, because I felt they'd embrace me more. They did, and I created a buzz that impacted my mainstream work! I became known for bringing plus bodies into the music video world. Sometimes when we don't fit the mold of society, it causes our flame to go out because of the discouragement of not being accepted. This is where persistence kicks in. You must be willing to find your path. Know that everything placed in you has purpose and destiny associated with it. Don't let others' failure to understand the vastness of who you are put your fire out.

> *"Make it work!"*
> *– Tim Gunn*

MAKE IT WORK

If you are a fan of *Project Runway*, you've heard Tim Gunn's oft-quoted phrase, "Make it Work!" I just love

Tim Gunn! No matter what your dreams are in life, you've got to persist and make it work for you. Regardless of who you are, you have to work with the hand you're dealt with and make it work for you. The truth is, you have all you need to be successful. Inside you is the power to make it work for your benefit. You must believe that.

I love being a plus-size woman, because it is who I am. I love being me. Sometimes being you is out of the norm. Sometimes who you are is out of the ordinary or goes against the grain. There are people who will take what you see as a blessing and see it as a limitation. This is where you have to persistently make your assets work for you.

I don't see being plus size as a limitation. Sometimes people say, "I just don't like calling you *plus size*," because they see the label as negative. They see it as something that feels bad. But this goes back to the old idea of perception. It feels bad to them, not to me. Plus means more. I am that! I am more—more than enough. *More* beautiful, *more* fabulous, *more* smart, *more* sexy. I am more! They may see it as a stigma, but I see it as beautiful, and I make it work! Honestly, plus is just a way for me to find my clothes. That's it. Because I am so clear about that, I refuse to let anything hinder me based on anyone else's limited scope of who I am and what is available to me. I make my extra work for me, honey.

Every Cloud Has a Silver Lining

Are you willing to persist despite the challenges? You should, because every cloud has a silver lining. We all face difficulties in life. What makes the difference is how we see them. How we process our adversity is of greatest importance. Will you be the one who looks at problems and sees opportunities? Every pain has promise within it. There are opportunities for you to learn and to grow and to be bigger and better than you were before you entered the storm. Persistence demands that you look for the good. If you don't, you will give up. No one can tolerate suffering forever. You can make it! I want you to win!

Learn from Your Pain

I want you to think about the most difficult or frustrating time in your life. Maybe it was the loss of your marriage. Perhaps it was the end of your dream job. It could have been even something as devastating as the death of a loved one. Are you still here? Yes! So even though you went through that most difficult hardship of your life, you are still here! That alone bears witness to your determination. Now I want you to look at that experience and take some time to see what good came out of it.

Did you learn that even though your marriage ended in a horrible fashion, you discovered the ability to forgive? Did you lose that dream job but found out there was something you loved even more than that and was far more rewarding too? Even with the loss of your loved one, were you able to look back with a smile at the joyful memories you had? Could you choose to remember the great times you shared? Were you able to see that grief would not keep you stuck? No matter what you have gone through, there is goodness in it. Find the silver lining. Learn from the pain. Look for the blessings.

It's Growth Time

Embrace every opportunity to learn and grow. Sometimes they come disguised as trouble, yet we stretch, grow through them, and become more of who we really are. When I moved to New York, I stayed with family. After a short while, I realized I needed to be on my own. The industry I was in meant that there were late nights, and my older family members did not quite understand the hours I kept. I had to make a change. I had to leap. I had no money, but I went out anyway. There are so many lessons I learned in this process. I learned I could survive on very little. It made me become very resourceful. Talk about recycling? I could do it. I learned to live with other people. Growing up, although I have a sister, she was much older than I am, so I grew up mostly as an only child. Not in this season. I had roommate after roommate. It made me grow up and really learn how to communicate effectively. It was challenging to say the least, but it was a learning experience that has allowed me to be the confident communicator I am today.

Look at your life and see your growth spurts. Remember when you would see loved ones after some time? They'd always swear you'd grown five inches since they'd last seen you. They would ask your parents what they were feeding you. I'll bet your valley seasons preceded your greatest internal growth spurts.

Runway Action Plan—Ask Yourself...

Grab your journal. You know.

I want you to think about the lessons you've learned just in the last year. Remember that thing that brought you to your knees.

— What made you cry all night long?

— What did you learn?

— How did your character develop?

Write them down. This is the power of a journal. It's interesting how when we keep a record of them and go back and read them later, it lets us know we were on the right track. Success is in reach. That adds to your confidence. It inspires you to keep going and to persist until you reach your goals.

HANG IN THERE FOR THE LONG HAUL

Some final words on persistence. Life is a marathon. It certainly is not a sprint. We all want to be here for a long, long time. The funny thing is that we don't act like that when it comes to our success. We live in a microwave society. We don't want things in a New York second—we want them yesterday. Life doesn't work like that. It's taken me a long time to build the career I have, but I was in it for the long haul. You must settle that in your mind and heart. It's interesting that even with my being on *Project Runway*, some people thought I was this new model on the block, not realizing that I have been modeling for over a decade already. Most overnight successes have taken decades.

To me, it really didn't matter how long it took. I was willing to keep striking at it until I struck gold and reached my goals. You must have the same persistence as well. Many times, things will not happen when we want them to. We have to be willing to trust that we are in the right place at the right time and that everything is coming together in divine timing. I know we have all heard that God is never early. That's the truth. He's never late, even though it may not feel like it sometimes. He's right on time. Do we believe that?

> *"Why are you trying to fit in when*
> *you were born to stand out!"*
> *— Unknown*

"Be so good they can't ignore you."
– Steve Martin

STAND OUT!

Finally, on your runway of life, you must always look for how you can make a name for yourself so that you can stand out. That has always been in the forefront of my thinking. Be your own advocate. How can you expect anyone else to believe in you or promote you if you don't? No matter what you're doing, you must be persistent and working to be the very best at it so that when people think of whatever it is that you do, they think of you first. Stand out. Make a name for yourself.

Runway Story Time

All throughout my career, I did not rely on agents alone to represent me or as the only way to generate income. I represent myself every single day. I rely on God and me being the best agent for me. I'm responsible for selling myself. The agent may get the casting, but I still have to go and knock it out of the park. I've still got to go in there and sell myself to the client so that they must have me. I need to stand out. How about with you? Your job may set up the appointment for the sales meeting, but you have to present yourself in such a way that the client wants to buy whatever it is you're selling too. You must close the deal.

So how will you make a name for yourself? Here's what I did. Even though I was signed with one of the biggest agencies in the world, I also knew I could have an impact in the urban modeling world, which was the video vixen market and working with urban brands like Fubu, Enyce, Mecca, and Karl Kani. These were brands that would have clothing with a little stretch or cut that can handle my marvelous curves. I also felt like they would be more open to using a woman of color. I wanted to be the model that stood out among the vast sea of straight-size models.

Have your pitch. I sold myself to companies by saying, "If you want a look that has more curves or something a little different for your brand, book me!" I went in there with the same confidence as those models who wore a size 2. There's nothing you could say to me to make me think I was less than them, because I was more. Persistence says where there is a will, there is a way. In truth, the way is made by the persistence itself. Stay at it. Instead of saying that it can't work, ask yourself, *How can it work?* Stay persistent, my friend.

Runway Action Plan

Have your journal? Let's go.

If you haven't answered the passion and pain questions earlier in the chapter, please do so. These questions are designed to give yourself an action plan for what you will do when you hit a roadblock and disappointments and want to give up.

When you feel like quitting, remember...

— What is your BIG why?

— How can you grow from this challenge?

— What is God trying to tell you?

— Who else needs you to succeed in this right now? Why?

— If you give up, who else might give up?

— How are you going to change your physical state so that you feel better right now?

— What can you do to shift your mental state?

— Who can you go help right now?

— Who can you call for a lift me up?

— What speaker can you listen to?

— What book or books can you read?

— What are five quotes that will remind you that you are bigger than your pain?

Got the idea? You may hit snags in your plans, and that's okay. Plan for how to come out of them in advance, passionately and persistently.

*"The most common way people give up their power
is by thinking they don't have any."*
– Alice Walker

*"We're here for a reason. I believe a bit of the
reason is to throw little torches out to lead people
through the dark."*
– Whoopi Goldberg

*"As iron sharpens iron, so one person sharpens
another."*
– Proverbs 27:17

— 6 —

STAND IN YOUR POWER AND BUILD PARTNERSHIPS

POWER IS BEING ABLE TO HAVE AN IMPACT. People mistake true power with just fame and riches, but power is available to and inherent in everyone. The young woman who's a cashier at Chick-fil-A has the same capability to stand in her power as the popular television show host. The TV host has power because they're able to give stories and to share information. To the person who is hungry and not in a great mood, the sunny, cheerful disposition of the young woman who waits on them, fills their order correctly, and sends them off feeling a little lighter has stood in her power to positively affect another's day.

You don't have to be rich or famous to have power, but what you do have to do to use your power is to recognize it and stand fully in it. Know what you bring to the table. All of that is important. People crave power, and people respect power. It's evident in popular culture. There's even a highly watched TV show called *Power*. It just shows you how important power is in our day-to-day lives.

PRIORITIES AND BOUNDARIES!

How do you communicate your true power to yourself? I believe that making yourself a priority gives you power. Many times, as women, we put ourselves on the bottom of our list. We discount ourselves and take from our own power. Who cares if other people see you as powerful if within you feel powerless? We have been socialized to put everyone and everything before us and told that that makes us a good woman. Subconsciously, it communicates that we are not as important as the roles we play.

Years ago, Iyanla Vanzant was a staple on *The Oprah Winfrey Show*. Unfortunately, there was a breach in their relationship, and they went their separate ways for years. Before the talk show ended, they came together on the show to discuss what happened and to try to come to a mutual understanding in front of us all. One of the things that was so compelling was Iyanla said, "I didn't think you wanted me." Oprah replied how ridiculous that was because she had given up her whole platform on a weekly basis for Iyanla to share her gifts. What she didn't know was that Iyanla felt like Oprah just wanted the work she did, but she didn't really want her as a person. You cannot stand in your power when you feel unworthy of it or if you only see the value in your gifts and not in you as a person. You are valuable. You are worthy, whether you do another thing inherently or not, and you are a person of worth, value, and substance. To internalize that truth, you have to make yourself a priority. You must put yourself at the top of the list. It is the old "put your oxygen mask on first" wisdom. Put yours on first, and then you can help others put theirs on too.

PLUG THE DRAINS

Recently, I was talking to a business associate. She explained how people call on her for certain things that are so draining to her. She acknowledged she needed to do better about setting boundaries, and commented how she thought I seem to be pretty good at that. The truth is that it has been a process. I have grown into being much better about it.

Set boundaries. The very thought of it can strike fear in our hearts of the disapproval or disappointment of others, but you must love yourself enough to do it. Love yourself enough to know that if you don't take care of yourself first, you can't be a great service to others. Know that you deserve your own time. You deserve peace. You deserve to clock out when you need to. You deserve to be engaged when you desire to. It's your prerogative to plug up any power drains in your life. You don't have to allow people to sap all your energy. If you are not right, you can't help anyone else—especially yourself.

Runway Story Time—Stay within the Lines

Every runway has boundaries. In my Life of a Working Model Boot Camp, I always create a fake runway by putting painter's tape on the floor. Then I instruct the participants they are to walk straight ahead, with their heads up, using their runway awareness as they are walking down the created runway.

When you first come out, you are off to one side. At the end of the runway you come toward the middle in order to take your picture. Then you need to share the runway and move to the opposite side as you're leaving and another model is coming on. At all times, you must make sure your placement in the space is correct. If you step on or beyond the tape, you have fallen off the runway. I call it *runway awareness.*

The same holds true in the runway of life. You must have life awareness with regard to your boundaries. Know who's draining you. Pay attention to when your tank is not full or close to empty. Be aware of your surroundings and how they are affecting you. Be conscious of your body and your mind and how it is affecting you. Know when they're getting to the edge. Pay attention to when people are pushing you to the edge. Strive to be awake and fully aware of where you are in your life, in relationship to others and the circumstances of your life. Be mindful of when you need to rest. Take time to renew yourself. Set loving boundaries that will protect and preserve you and sustain your sanity. If you do not, it will drain you of your power, and you won't have anyone else to blame. This is your responsibility. Preserve your power.

"No" Is a Complete Sentence

This may feel harsh, but trust me, it is not. You have to say NO sometimes. And there are times when *no* is a complete sentence. End of story. No explanation is needed. It's just, no. If you don't, people will deplete you. You cannot serve from an empty cup. To benefit others and to make the world your runway so you can impact the world in a way that only you can, build yourself first. That requires telling people no. Everything operates from within you first. *No* is not always *never*; it may just be *not right now*. When you are at the top of your list, then you can say YES to what is based on your purpose and goals.

LESS IS MORE

When I walk to the end of a runway in a show, I know I have three seconds to offer an amazing picture. I stand in whatever pose I decide to do powerfully. There is no place for indecision on the runway. My thought is "Hey, world! Look at me. Take a bit of me. Love on me. Accept my offering. Appreciate this moment of time with me."

When you walk into a room, decisively stand in the power of who you are. Many times, when I am teaching on the runway, I notice how ladies will come down the runway and do their pose so quickly. Then they rush off the runway, and the photographer is not even able to get a great shot of them. No, no, no. To be the powerful, confident woman that you are, linger a little. Take your time. Stand in the power of your moment. Allow others the joy of taking you in. Don't rush it. I see this sometimes in speakers, teachers, preachers, or just those in everyday communication. We can get in such a hurry to make the next point that we don't allow the present point to land. We can be so focused on the next project we don't acknowledge the power and accomplishments of the present project. Don't rush it. Take it in. Let others take it in. That infuses you and everyone else with power.

Other times on the runway, models can overdo it. They try to do too many poses in that short period of time. Often, all you need is one good strong pose. Sometimes we are just doing too much. Instead of focusing on one business, we are trying to launch three. Rather than prioritize building one skill, we think we can build ten skills at the same time. We are not realizing less is more. As a result, we become scattered and fearful, throwing anything and everything at the wall hoping something will stick.

Has that ever happened to you? You begin to feel hopeless because something you were excited about didn't work out. So instead of taking the time to analyze what might have happened, you jump from business to business, relationship to relationship, diet to diet. You're all over the place. Remember, life is a marathon. There is no rush. Relax. Take a deep breath. Gather yourself. Get focused. On the runway, I'm focused. A powerful person is keenly focused. Practice focusing on one to three major goals at a time if this is your struggle. Minimize your distractions so you don't try to spread yourself so thin that your power becomes diluted. Stay potent. We don't want a watered-down version of you. We want the real deal.

TELL YOUR STORY

We all have a story to tell, and there's power in it. Never be ashamed of where you've come from. Your entire journey was part of the beautiful tapestry of your life and has tremendous value to the world. When you tell your story, you can positively uplift and impact the lives of others—that's power. You are also reminding yourself of how far you've come. When you do this with a great sense of gratitude, that's power! When others can look at you and say, "Wow! You went through that too. I'm not alone in these streets," that gives them power to believe they can overcome as well. It allows others to gain the confidence to be okay with where they've been and what they've experienced too. Now, it empowers them to share their story, to lift someone else up and to strive for more. You have created a powerful ripple effect just by being vulnerable enough to tell your power story. This is why I love to pour into the lives of others and to share my own trials and triumphs. This fuels me to train the next generation of models who are taking the industry by storm. It is also why I wrote this book. I want my story to inspire you and cause you to walk in your own power.

"There are people who make things happen, there are people who watch things happen, and there are people who wonder what happened. To be successful, you need to be a person who makes things happen."
– Jim Lovell

*"I've always been attracted to women who are
assertive and have confidence—
qualities older women possess. They've been on the
Earth a little longer. They're more seasoned.
They don't play games. They know what they want,
and they're not afraid to tell you."*
– Taye Diggs

BE ASSERTIVE

Alright, Taye Diggs! Tell the truth. There is power in
being assertive. For my ladies, men love confident
women. I'm not talking about pushy, bitchy women; but
assertive, self-assured women are magnetic. There is
great power in knowing who you are and acting out of
it. An assertive woman reflects and responds. She is
polished and proactive. She knows what she is worthy of.
She knows what she deserves. Her standards are high,
and she keeps them there. And she will convey her
standards unapologetically.

An assertive woman makes things happen. Especially
in business, people love that. They love to be around
someone who can and will make a decision. The same is
true of women. Women love a man who will stand up,
make a decision, and take action. He doesn't always have
to be right, but he ought to be moving in the right
direction.

On the runway of life, you must be assertive enough to ask for what you want. This is part of the reason why people turn to me for guidance. In the modeling industry, I have paid my dues. I know what I know. I'm sure about it. I'm confident in it. I know I can help you. I can support you in creating the career you desire and the life you want the most.

Know what you know. If you know you are an excellent parent, own that. If you know nobody can teach the way you do, know that. Only be involved in what you are passionate about and fully believe in. When you do, it becomes evident to everyone else. You don't have to convince anybody that you know anything. You don't have to lead them into believing anything. You just need to show them that you believe it. That's the power of influence and walking in true confidence and assertiveness. They just need to believe that *you* believe it. People listen to people who believe. Again, an assertive woman is a mover and a shaker. She uses her power to get things done.

What if you don't feel that way yet? Again, let me reiterate this. Fake it until you make it. I've had to do that many times. I sometimes cringe at that word "fake" because what it really means is to FAITH it until you make it. Eventually, your feelings will follow your faith. Act as if. Deep down inside, the "real you" really *is* assertive, confident, and self-assured. Act as if until your feelings catch up. They will. Faith draws from the unseen to make it seen. Step out in faith.

Runway Story Time

Many times, early in my career, I would be the thickest girl on the set of a video or movie. Because I always aim to be prepared, I have packed my own bag of outfits to wear. I made sure that I controlled how I was going to look. They would not be able to just stick me in a bikini in a scene where that doesn't even make sense, just because they didn't have anything to fit me.

Even if I was booked as just an extra, because of my assertive aura I often became a featured person in the video. I made you notice me by how I carried myself and by the outfit I wore. I asserted myself into the scene. I carried myself like I was the star, even though I was an extra. Here's the key. When you believe you are a star, others will start to believe it too. The funny thing is I would often be featured as a lead person even though I wasn't booked as one. They didn't know it before they booked me, but I was the star. Faith it until you make it.

Runway Action Plan—Ask Yourself…

Grab your journal. Let's go!

Let's hit this right between the eyes. It's time to plug up those power drains. Ask yourself…

— Who in my life is a constant drain?

— What things am I currently doing that I despise and are not taking me where I want to go?

— What are things I have said yes to that I know I should have said no to?

— Who am I going to call in the next forty-eight hours to say no to?

— What boundaries do I need to send in order to preserve my own sanity?

— Who is the person that I am most afraid to say no to?

— What *no* do I need to tell them right now?

— What are five things that I'm going to say yes to right now to preserve my own power?

Trust me. Doing this will not be easy, but it will be so worth it. Preserve your power.

PARTNERSHIPS

"You can't become yourself all by yourself."
– Karin Haysbert

"If you want to go fast, go alone. If you want to go far, go together."
– African proverb

"Two people are better off than one, for they can help each other succeed."
– Ecclesiastes 4:9

Our lives succeed or fail based on the quality of our relationships. Partnerships are important because we all need others in our lives. No one is an island. We were made to be interconnected and interdependent. It has been said that a draft horse can pull eight thousand pounds alone, but when you yoke him beside another horse, the two can pull twenty-four thousand pounds together. That is the power of partnerships. We have all heard that it takes a village to raise a child. Honestly, it takes a village to raise anyone to another level in life. For any of us to become the best of who we are, it always takes relationships.

There is beauty in singleness, but there's a special strength that is also in marriage. The passage in Ecclesiastes says that two are better than one because you can help one another to succeed. It goes on to say that "if one person falls, the other can reach out and help, but someone who falls alone is in real trouble." If you are trying to live this life all alone, on your own, you are headed for trouble. Truthfully, a confident person never lives that way. We understand not just the value in ourselves but also the value in others as well. We know that we need to rub up against others to be our best. Iron sharpens iron.

YOUR PERSONAL TRIBE

Who's in your personal tribe? I believe it is vitally important to have people in your tribe who are on the same journey as you are. You understand what each other is going through, so you can lend support and be a source of encouragement for one another. It's also great to be able to bounce ideas off one another, to brainstorm or mastermind with each other. You can help to push each other.

Check the various areas of your life. Who's there? Some people have workout partners for your gym goals. Perhaps you have a go-to friend who you can talk about marriage or singlehood with. You may have a parents' group where you support one another. Of course, there are business relationships where you can support each other in growing your craft. What about the person who is just inspiration on fire to you? And everyone needs someone who gives love to you like Grandma's hugs. Who are you to others? Lastly, how can you hold each other accountable?

WHO'S POURING INTO YOUR LIFE?

Please understand the value of mentors in your partnerships with people who are further along than you are. You can have mentors who are up close and those who are from afar. On a spiritual and personal level, one of my greatest mentors is my sister, Karin Haysbert. She is a wife, mentor, minister, author, and life coach. Because of our age gap, I often joke that she is the test dummy for my life, LOL. I'm often able to see her go through the ups and downs of life and overcome in certain areas that prove to be so beneficial for me. What's beautiful is she always continues to navigate life by learning, growing, and changing. She is always expanding as a person. She is still the Karin I grew up with, but she's an even more evolved, beautiful version of herself. I love being able to have long discussions with her and to see how she sees the world and life. I so appreciate that.

Another great mentor is celebrity fashion stylist and author Susan Moses. She has been in the fashion industry for over twenty years. She's worked with a variety of clients, including straight-size and plus-size celebrities. She's been known to style some of the top plus-size actresses and musical artists. Susan has been a master at reinventing herself too. She has been instrumental in pushing the plus fashion culture forward over the years. She's written her own book, *The Art of Dressing Curves*, which I highly recommend. She has been a huge contributor to the world of fashion, much more than I think many even realize. Susan absolutely knows the business. It's a blessing to have a relationship with her, because she is someone who I have worked for and with. I respect her advice and her insight. There were times in my career when she could sense I was just tired. She has had a way of helping to push me forward, giving me the strength to keep going. I love being able to just have sister girl talks with her too. We'll share stories and it's like, "Wow, you've been through that too?" It's wonderful to not feel alone when you know that you are not the only one experiencing this. Susan blesses my life in that way.

I have several friends also who pour into me and inspire me. I look up to my guy bestie and fashion designer, William Rawls. He loves God. He loves people. He loves fashion. As a designer, he has a different perspective on the industry that I find so refreshing and beneficial. His creativity gives me life, and he has this awesome way of giving me the other side of the coin so I can look at life from a different perspective. Pervis Taylor also encourages and inspires me. He is a phenomenal celebrity life coach, author, and speaker— and my friend. We first connected because we were both in the entertainment industry pursuing acting. We have been friends for over a decade. It's beautiful to get perspective from a black man who is emotionally present. He's a great supporter and has always had my back. He knows me for who I truly am. Markita Collins has been such a blessing to my life. She is a powerful minister, author, and coach. Markita is a newer friendship for me. In ways, she is stronger than I am spiritually, and I'm thankful for how she pulls me up to higher heights in the spiritual realm. You need people like that in your life. Then there's my best friend forever, Christy Baldwin. I just love her so much. She knows me, and she loves me unconditionally for who I am. I also appreciate how she is not afraid to tell me the truth, whether it's good or bad. Everyone needs truth-tellers in their Inner Circle.

Hang out with people in three different levels of life. Always have mentors. They are those who are where you wish to be. You may have close mentors, like those I mentioned, or those who mentor you from afar, like Oprah, Dr. King, or Mother Teresa. Let their lives mentor you. Even biographies of great leaders can serve as a source of mentorship for you. Nurture your friendships. They are people who are where you are. You're on about the same level. You understand one another and are going in the same direction. Lastly, have protegees. You must give back. Protegees are those who want to be where you are. Pour into their lives. Pull them up. Be an example for them. Be the gift to them that so many have been to you.

POSITIVE PARTNERSHIPS

Surround yourself with positive partnerships. This may seem obvious, but let me explain. I spoke in a previous chapter about immersing yourself in the culture of your purpose. It's important to have positive partnerships that support the work-life culture you are creating. You gain information and insight. This is how you grow and gain new opportunities. It's how you change and elevate.

Be intentional about how you can add value in your relationships with others. I have a model friend named

Naimah Terry. We are both plus models, but we have totally different looks. We will reach out to one another and share information about jobs and castings. I may see a job that she's more suited for and vice versa. We will pass it on to one another. That is the type of network we have built, where we each support one another and help to put food on each other's tables. It's important to have unselfish relationships with others. When they win, you win. When you win, they win. It's always win-win. I have found that reciprocal relationships can be the most rewarding.

Additionally, let's take it a step further. Surround yourself with people who celebrate your successes. You need those positive relationships in your life. It's a confidence boost when you know you have people who love, appreciate, and celebrate you in your life. It feels good to have people who have your back and your best interests at heart. I have created partnerships with people who are not in the fashion industry who have proved to be fruitful as well. You never know who may hear about something where a company or individual is looking for someone just like you for their project.

Find ways to positively impact others. There have been people who I have only worked with once or twice, but I noticed they were excellent at what they did. Their passion is magnetic. I'll hold on to their information, and if I hear about anything that might work for them, I'll send it to them. They so appreciate that gesture. That makes them remember me. I aim to treat people the way I desire to be treated. Live by the golden rule in your business relationships. Entrepreneurship is not for the faint of heart. We must support one another. Often, when you finish one job, you're unemployed until you get the next job. Think of others. Plant good seeds that will spring up for you later. Sow for your own success.

BE COMPLEMENTARY

You want to have complementary relationships. I have learned to stay in my lane. Just because you can do something, it doesn't mean that you should. You may have heard the phrase *staffing your weakness.* In business, you should never try to do everything yourself all the time (although I do feel it's smart to know how to work every position). You're just not good at everything, so to compensate for your weaknesses, hire someone. Staff it. This is an area I had to grow in as my brand has expanded. It takes a level of trust that I'm still learning, but I must say it's worth it to staff it, LOL!

How about in your relationships? If you have an area of weakness, why not surround yourself with people who are strong in that area? Learn from them. If you are struggling with eating healthy, don't hang around people who are also struggling in that same area. Connect with someone who has a great healthy lifestyle and diet. You can observe them. You can ask them questions. You can get a good sense of why they live the way they do and how you may adopt some of their mindset and practices. By the same token, you should have something to offer them as well. Look for complementary relationships. Relationships that give and receive are the best.

BE A GREAT GIVER

Let's dive deeper into giving. Live with open hands and an open heart. When your hands are closed, nothing can get out of them, but nothing can get into them either. I've learned the power of sowing good seeds and the power in giving. The more I give, the more I have to give. My life is in a constant flow of good when I aim to bless more than to be blessed. It's a spiritual law that always proves true. Surround yourself with people who have liberal hearts too, but it all begins with you.

> *"Everyone you meet is fighting a battle you know nothing about. Be kind. Always."*
> *– Brad Meltzer*

BE KIND. ALWAYS.

Be kind. Give kindness and random acts of kindness whenever you can. When you're on the runway, all eyes are on you. Live your life as if all eyes are on you. Always give your very best, and treat people with lovingkindness. How you treat people will always be reflected back to you. It is also a representation of your character. I find that how you treat people who can't give you something in return says a lot about you. How do you treat the doorman, the waiter, or the maid? Each are noble positions of service. Do you look down on them, or do you see the wonder in who they are too? I remember being on a date with a seemingly great guy who treated the taxi cab driver with such disdain for no reason at all. The taxi driver was not rude or unkind to him. That was the last time he saw me. I refuse to give time or attention to people who treat strangers with such disrespect. If you do that to a stranger who has done you no wrong, you'll do worse to someone close to you when you're having a bad day. Being kind may not happen all the time, but if you make it your aim, it will happen much more than not. Be kind. Always.

Your Network Affects Your Net Worth

They say that it's not always what you know but who you know that makes the difference. Networking is vital. Connect with others through their social media, through their business card, or via email. Here's a time when simple networking proved to be very profitable to me.

Runway Story Time

Last year, my best friend, Christy, was getting married. We went out shopping for her bridal gown to the premiere plus-size-only bridal boutique in the US, located right in my hometown in Maryland, called Curvaceous Couture Bridal. While we were there, one of the owners was there too. My best friend told them who I was, that I was a plus-size model and had appeared on *Project Runway*. Christy urged me to give them my comp card, which is a model's business card that displays a variety pictures of you and your contact information. A lot of times there are not a lot of paying jobs for models in Baltimore, but I thought, you never know if there is something I could lend my expertise to that could lead to something profitable. Here again, be a giver. This is a practice of networking I established very early in my career, always handing out business cards. I networked wherever I was, even at the club. I was the girl who had just graduated from high school and was trying to connect with everyone for work. I still have that fire now.

So I got the owner's email information and sent her my comp card. Little did I know that she had something in the works. That "chance meeting" occurred in the summer. I say *chance*, but nothing happens by chance. Everything is orchestrated. Toward the end of the year, my agent called me saying that a client wanted to put me on hold for a job. It wasn't a client I had ever worked with before. I never even attended a casting, and they booked me. It was Maggie Sottero.

When I went to the job for Maggie Sottero, I asked them how they found out about me. They said they have been working diligently to expand their plus-size market. They contacted the ladies at one of their favorite boutiques, Curvaceous Couture Bridal. They asked them who they thought they should use, and the ladies told them they should use me. Wow. Mind you, I had never worked with Curvaceous Couture Bridal. Their only exposure to me was when I met them that one day in the boutique. I'm sure I must have made a positive impression on them then, and the fact that I followed up just like I said I would helped too. Little did I know that my following through on this meeting would turn into working with one of my favorite clients. Now, I am an exclusive spokesperson for Maggie Sottero Designs across the world. That's huge! It came from just sending an email.

And, finally, say thank you. I made sure that I sent the owner at Curvaceous Couture Bridal a beautiful bouquet to express my gratitude.

You don't know who's watching you. You never know what opportunities are hidden in everyday circumstances. This huge opportunity came from just planting a small seed. A seed could be sending a text, forwarding an email, or adding someone on Instagram. When you are kind to others, someone will see you and refer you to someone else. You have no idea how it will come back to you. Always be your best. Always do your best. Always treat others with kindness and respect. Always network.

Network and Nurture

Network, nurture, and follow through. Send out birthday wishes. Email your updated resume to your contacts. When you make a great connection with someone, even if they do not select you for the job, stay in contact. Check in with them every few months. If it's your dream job, another position may open up. Maybe you are an artist and you weren't able to be a part of a certain gallery. If you keep in contact with them, and they are able to see your growth, they may extend the opportunity later. Stay connected. It may have just not been your season. Sometimes you will see it on the competition shows. The judges see the raw talent, and they suggest that they go home and refine their skills a little more so they can come back and try again. Take that advice. Go work on yourself. Come back better. Come back more developed in your skills. Sharpen your saw.

Add a Little Contrast to Your Life

This world is full of very diverse cultures and peoples. Add a little contrast to your life. Not everyone in your life should think the same way as you do. I think that is the beauty of travel. You get to experience different cultures and to view how other people see the world. It helps us to create an appreciation for humankind. If everyone is telling you that everything you do is perfect and amazing, you need to expand your circle. Just saying.

Here's how I add a little contrast and a little sizzle to my circle. On social media, I might follow a liberal, a conservative, and an independent. I like to learn how all these people have varying views. Just because someone is different from you, it doesn't mean they're wrong, and it doesn't mean you can't appreciate their point of view. I'm a Christian, but I can follow someone who is Muslim or Buddhist. It's so important for us to have common respect for people. When we can respect humankind, we operate in the world with greater power and impact. You don't have to agree with everyone to be able to relate to them. You can have respect and compassion for their point of view.

"I'm an ambitious person. I never considered myself in competition with anyone, and I'm not saying that from an arrogant standpoint. It's just that my journey started so, so long ago, and I'm still on it, and I won't stand still."
– Idris Elba

"Women compete. Queens collaborate."
– Karin Haysbert

DITCH COMPETITION

A couple of years ago my sister told me something about
sisterhood. She said, "Women compete. Queens
collaborate." I love that! Partnership and collaboration
are so important because we all have different things we
bring to the table. I really feel this is key in making the
world your runway. There is such beauty in our
differences. When we all come together and partner up,
it's like making the most beautiful, colorful bouquet of
flowers. We all shine in different hues.

We're so much alike, but we are all different too. I
love Idris. He's a dear friend. He's right. Our
perspectives are different. Our life journeys differ.
Because of that, even if you do the same thing I do, you
can't do it like I do it. There really is no competition
when we are being our authentic selves. Competition
also has an undercurrent of fear and lack in it. It makes
it seem like if you win, I lose. It comes from the feeling
that there is not enough for everyone. That is simply not
true. This universe overflows with abundance. When I
changed my mind-set to believe God will create
opportunities for those of us willing to believe,
everything changed for me. We just have to do our part
and wish to spread love and beauty in the world through
our gifts together. Collaborate. The world was never
meant to be monotone. It's made much like a symphony
of many different instruments, each with its own sound.

But when we come together, we make one beautiful, harmonious sound.

In Closing

Making the World Your Runway

Congratulations! You made it to the end. It has been my honor to share with you these tools for your greater confidence and success to make the world your runway. Whether it is discovering and living in your purpose or polishing your physical presentation and becoming more positive in your thoughts and words, I trust that you gleaned practical strategies to transform your life.

ABOUT LIRIS

I am a keynote speaker and speak at and conduct workshops and conferences for fashion and entertainment industry events, business and entrepreneurial communities, and for events with women and teen girls for church groups and spiritual organizations. I am an expert in the areas of breaking into the modeling industry, perfection in pose, mastering your modeling craft, creating longevity in the modeling industry, making the world your runway, inner confidence, and body confidence. Email me to book me at your next conference or event. Let's make the world your runway! Thank you!

Want to go further? There's nothing like working with me live! For more information on how to attend my Life of a Working Model Bootcamps, to book me for a Make the World Your Runway Workshop, or for the most up-to-date information on where I am modeling, acting, or speaking, here's how to connect with me:

WEBSITE: www.LirisC.com

EMAIL: booklirisc@gmail.com

FACEBOOK: www.facebook.com/lirisc

YOUTUBE: www.youtube.com/loawmodel

INSTAGRAM: www.instagram.com/lirisc

Many blessings,

Liris C